New Directions for Community Colleges

Arthur M. Cohen
EDITOR-IN-CHIEF

Caroline Q. Durdella
Nathan R. Durdella
ASSOCIATE EDITORS

Amy Fara Edwards
MANAGING EDITOR

Promising and High-Impact Practices: Student Success Programs in the Community College Context

Gloria Crisp
Deryl K. Hatch

EDITORS

Number 175 • Fall 2016
Jossey-Bass
San Francisco

PROMISING AND HIGH-IMPACT PRACTICES: STUDENT SUCCESS PROGRAMS IN THE COMMUNITY COLLEGE
CONTEXT
Gloria Crisp, Deryl K. Hatch (eds.)
New Directions for Community Colleges, no. 175

Arthur M. Cohen, Editor-in-Chief
Caroline Q. Durdella, Nathan R. Durdella, Associate Editors
Amy Fara Edwards, Managing Editor

NEW DIRECTIONS FOR COMMUNITY COLLEGES (ISSN 0194-3081, electronic ISSN 1536-0733) is part of The Jossey-Bass Higher and Adult Education Series and is published quarterly by Wiley Subscription Services, Inc., A Wiley Company, at Jossey-Bass, One Montgomery St., Ste. 1200, San Francisco, CA 94104. POSTMASTER: Send address changes to New Directions for Community Colleges, Jossey-Bass, One Montgomery St., Ste. 1200, San Francisco, CA 94104.

SUBSCRIPTIONS cost $89 for individuals in the U.S., Canada, and Mexico, and $113 in the rest of the world for print only; $89 in all regions for electronic only; $98 in the U.S., Canada, and Mexico for combined print and electronic; $122 for combined print and electronic in the rest of the world. Institutional print only subscriptions are $335 in the U.S., $375 in Canada and Mexico, and $409 in the rest of the world; electronic only subscriptions are $335 in all regions; combined print and electronic subscriptions are $402 in the U.S., $442 in Canada and Mexico, and $476 in the rest of the world.

Cover design: Wiley
Cover Images: © Lava 4 images | Shutterstock

EDITORIAL CORRESPONDENCE should be sent to the Editor-in-Chief, Arthur M. Cohen, at 1749 Mandeville Lane, Los Angeles, CA 90049. All manuscripts receive anonymous reviews by external referees.

New Directions for Community Colleges is indexed in CIJE: Current Index to Journals in Education (ERIC), Contents Pages in Education (T&F), Current Abstracts (EBSCO), Ed/Net (Simpson Communications), Education Index/Abstracts (H. W. Wilson), Educational Research Abstracts Online (T&F), ERIC Database (Education Resources Information Center), and Resources in Education (ERIC).

Microfilm copies of issues and articles are available in 16mm and 35mm, as well as microfiche in 105mm, through University Microfilms Inc., 300 North Zeeb Road, Ann Arbor, MI 48106-1346.

Contents

Editors' Notes

National reform movements have placed considerable attention and pressure on community colleges to substantially and efficiently increase the number of students who earn degrees and certificates in the next decade (Harbour, 2015). The Completion Agenda, led largely by policy makers, professional organizations, and philanthropic foundations, is a national imperative and democratic obligation to increase completion rates, collect quality data regarding students' pathways, and enact and improve policies that encourage and improve degree production. Though the aims of such an effort are welcome by community college practitioners and fit with these institutions' long-standing missions of community responsiveness, some warn that without accompanying means to ensure high quality, the Completion Agenda threatens to detract from open access, exacerbate inequities, and narrow the community college mission around their credentialing function (Lester, 2014).

Currently, about 39% of all students who enroll in community colleges obtain a degree or certificate at any institution within 6 years (Shapiro et al., 2015), whereas completion rates remain disproportionately lower for low-income students and students from underrepresented racial/minority groups. In response, the American Association of Community Colleges (AACC) has partnered with other national organizations in committing to assist community colleges in increasing the number of degrees and certificates earned by students by 50% by 2020. The AACC recommends that community college degree completion rates can be improved in part by enhancing "high-impact, evidence-based" educational practices such as orientations and first-year experience courses and by creating additional programs to engage students. Recent reports also urge colleges to reduce use of boutique programs and move toward bringing effective programs to scale (AACC, 2011, 2012).

The community college has unique characteristics that make identifying high-impact and potentially transferable practices a considerable challenge (Haberler & Levin, 2014). Community colleges are grounded by a fundamental mission to provide educational opportunity to students regardless of their prior academic experiences, ability to pay, or intentions to complete a degree program (Harbour, 2015). In support of the open access mission, community colleges strive to provide programs and services at a low cost, effectively restricting resources—absent additional public allocations—for specialized practices and programs that may support more students in formulating and realizing their ambitions (Mellow & Heelan, 2008).

Scholars agree that national completion goals cannot be achieved without community colleges substantially ramping up efforts to support success for the diversity of students who are enrolling at colleges. At the same time, community college stakeholders are searching with urgency for the magic potion of effective practice that will substantially increase completion rates for students of all backgrounds (Levin, Cox, Cerven, & Haberler, 2010; Weiss et al., 2014). Unfortunately, there are presently critical gaps in our understanding regarding how to effectively design and implement scalable practices and programs on community college campuses for such a wide variety of students.

This volume of *New Directions for Community Colleges* presents a compendium of the latest research and practice regarding practices and programs that researchers have identified as promising in fostering positive community college student outcomes. Our volume explores the latest research on how student success program research is conceptualized and operationalized and offers evidence for ways in which programs foster positive student outcomes, including ways that outcomes are defined in the first place beyond persistence, transfer, and credential attainment. The issue also provides a critical inquiry of how students themselves experience practices and programs and discusses challenges surrounding program design, implementation and evaluation. The volume brings together perspectives from researchers and administrators representing centers and federally funded projects seeking to build knowledge around promising practices and programs in community colleges, including the Community College Research Center (CCRC), Achieving the Dream, the Center for Community College Student Engagement (CCCSE) and the National Resource Center for The First-Year Experience and Students in Transition.

The issue begins with four chapters that offer frameworks for conceptualizing and understanding practices and programs on community college campuses. In Chapter 1, Deryl K. Hatch, Gloria Crisp, and Katherine Wesley summarize definitions for proposed high-impact programs and practices, relationships among them, and the kinds of impacts they are designed to achieve. This chapter offers a visual map to illustrate key relationships and program features. Next, Hatch offers a brief history of how various *special* or *high-impact* practices and programs have been identified and grouped as such, followed by an explanation of how Cultural Historical Activity Theory (CHAT) can be used as a framework for conceptualizing some of the more prominent kinds of student-success programs—at least those that are typically course based and go by a wide variety of labels—as instances of a more general type of intervention. Chapter 3, by Melinda Mechur Karp, senior research associate at the CCRC, invites readers to go beyond the idea of program containers and consider the fundamental *mechanisms* of nonacademic support that foster successful outcomes for community college students. Karp makes a case for how these mechanisms can be part of formally structured programs or implemented through other means—especially in-class interactions. Chapter 4, by Evelyn N. Waiwaiole, E. Michael Bohlig, and Kristine J. Massey of the CCCSE, describes how community colleges have been successful in leveraging CCCSE's High-Impact Practice (HIP) Institutes in developing and implementing short-term action plans to improve student outcomes. Examples of interventions that evolved from the institutes are provided as examples of how colleges can continue to use resources developed by CCCSE's HIP Initiative.

The next two chapters provide comparative and contextualized views of first-year experiences at community colleges. Chapter 5 is written by Dallin George Young and Jennifer R. Keup from the National Resource Center for The First-Year Experience and Students in Transition. Their work provides a national portrait of first-year seminars and their unique features in the community college setting in contrast to those found in 4-year institutions. Importantly, their chapter also shows how seminars serve as a place to connect students to other practices and programs that have been deemed high impact. The next chapter, by higher education scholars Nancy Acevedo-Gil and Desiree D. Zerquera, documents students' voices and perspectives in participating in community college first-year experience programs—a perspective that is sorely lacking in the national discussion and research literature related to high-impact practices.

The final three chapters of the volume are dedicated to providing practical advice, recommendations, and resources related to promising practices and programs at community colleges. In Chapter 7, Achieving the Dream Data Coaches, Bruce E. McComb and Jan W. Lyddon, offer guidance and best practices in evaluating student success interventions. Chapter 8, written by Vincent D. Carales, Crystal E. Garcia, and Naomi Mardock-Uman, identifies resources and relevant research to assist community college staff, faculty, and administrators in developing, implementing, and evaluating student success initiatives. Our volume concludes with a summary by Gloria Crisp of the key ideas and themes presented throughout the issue. She also provides observations and recommendations for future research regarding designing and implementing effective practices and programs at community colleges around the country.

Gloria Crisp
Deryl K. Hatch
Editors

New Directions for Community Colleges • DOI: 10.1002/cc

References

American Association of Community Colleges. (2011). *The completion agenda: A call to action*. Washington, DC: Author. Retrieved from http://www.aacc.nche.edu/ Publications/Reports/Documents/CompletionAgenda_report.pdf

American Association of Community Colleges. (2012). *Reclaiming the American dream: A report from the 21st-Century Commission on the Future of Community Colleges*. Washington, DC: Author. Retrieved from http://www.aacc.nche.edu/aboutcc/ 21stcenturyreport_old/index.html

Haberler, Z., & Levin, J. S. (2014). The four Cs of promising practices in community colleges. *Community College Journal of Research and Practice, 38*(5), 403–416. doi: 10.1080/10668926.2012.748381

Harbour, C. P. (2015). *John Dewey and the future of community college education*. London: Bloomsbury Academic.

Lester, J. (2014). The completion agenda: The unintended consequences for equity in community colleges. In M. B. Paulsen (Ed.), *Higher education: Handbook of theory and research* (Vol. 29, pp. 423–466). Dordrecht, the Netherlands: Springer.

Levin, J. S., Cox, E. M., Cerven, C., & Haberler, Z. (2010). The recipe for promising practices in community colleges. *Community College Review, 38*(1), 31–58.

Mellow, G. O., & Heelan, C. (2008). *Minding the dream: The process and practice of the American community college*. Lanham, MD: Roman & Littlefield.

Shapiro, D., Dundar, A., Wakhungu, P. K., Yuan, X., Nathan, A., & Hwang, Y. (2015). *Completing college: A national view of student attainment rates—Fall 2009 cohort* (Signature Report No. 10). Herndon, VA: National Student Clearinghouse Research Center.

Weiss, M. J., Mayer, A., Cullinan, D., Ratledge, A., Sommo, C., & Diamond, J. (2014). *A random assignment evaluation of learning communities at Kingsborough Community College: Seven years later*. New York, NY: MDRC.

GLORIA CRISP *is an associate professor, College of Education, Oregon State University at Corvallis, Oregon.*

DERYL K. HATCH *is an assistant professor of educational administration at the University of Nebraska–Lincoln.*

1

This chapter reviews multiple complementary and divergent descriptions of practices that have been identified as holding particular promise for high impact on college student success and offers a possible map of practices to illustrate key features and relationships.

What's in a Name? The Challenge and Utility of Defining Promising and High-Impact Practices

Deryl K. Hatch, Gloria Crisp, Katherine Wesley

In this chapter, we seek to lay groundwork for the remainder of the volume with what should be a straightforward task but in the end was among the more difficult aspects of compiling this volume: identifying and describing high-impact and promising practices. Rather than an exhaustive accounting of the ways practices have been grouped and defined (see Hatch, Chapter 2, for an abbreviated history), we frame our descriptions around what we see as key features that serve to both distinguish and connect practices and offer a map to illustrate these key features and relationships. In describing practices, we bring attention to what we see to be issues and considerations of complementary and divergent definitions for practice, research, and policy.

Issues/Limitations in Defining Programs and Practices

Defining high-impact practices is challenging because, ultimately, labels can reveal as much as they conceal about what goes into programs and practices (Hatch & Bohlig, 2016) and so we might do well to consider their impactful mechanisms instead (Karp, Chapter 3). The term *high impact* conveys the notion of a known gold standard of best practices when in fact what we call our best may "actually turn out to be none too good or not as good as we can do" (Kay McClenney, personal communication, June, 2010). Additionally, for practitioners and researchers alike, the term *high-impact practices* may inadvertently limit continued exploration of transformative educational practice or how key mechanisms of promising practices can be broadly integrated throughout college (Karp, Chapter 3).

New Directions for Community Colleges, no. 175, Fall 2016 © 2016 Wiley Periodicals, Inc.
Published online in Wiley Online Library (wileyonlinelibrary.com) • DOI: 10.1002/cc.20208

For instance, in conversations with instructional administrators, we learned that when implementing such promising practices, focus is typically given to tweaking elements of the practice to address local circumstances. This, in turn, may impede consideration of other possibilities beyond what the label implies and toward key mechanisms that might be broadly integrated throughout the college (Karp, Chapter 3). One example of how practices might be combined outside of programmatic labels is the emerging concept of guided pathways (Jenkins & Cho, 2013) in which multiple resources are brought to bear around a more deliberate and straightforward path to a credential or transfer instead of an overwhelming buffet of options and optional resources. Nonetheless, no matter how practices are designed, naming the ways particular college environments are created is unavoidable because labeling is fundamental to human nature and daily practice. We need working definitions at least as reference points.

Key Dimensions of High-Impact and Promising Practices

In broad terms, Levin, Cox, Cerven, and Haberler (2010) define educational practices at community colleges as "a specific form or way of organizing the educational experiences of individual students and college employees" (p. 35) and a *promising* instructional program as "one that has demonstrably improved student learning and has closed the achievement gap, as measured by course pass rates, certificate or degree attainment rates, and so forth" (p. 55). In Table 1.1, we bring together and describe practices and programs identified as "high impact" and/or "promising" by the Association of American Colleges & Universities (AAC&U) or the Center for Community College Student Engagement (CCCSE), or both (CCCSE, 2012; Kuh, 2008). We include other practices that have been shown to be positively related to student outcomes—for instance, bridge programs and mentoring (Crisp, 2010; Mitchell, Alozie, & Wathington, 2015)—that are conceptually related to named high-impact practices but not included on some lists. Both AAC&U and CCCSE's lists of programs and practices have shaped much of the recent conversation on student success programs and were therefore important to consider. Although not all of the practices identified by AAC&U may seem immediately relevant to a community college context (for instance, undergraduate research), we feel there may be worth in exploring their potential role in the community college sector as they are premised on means to foster college student success beyond measures of access, persistence, and completion—necessary but not sufficient—to "twenty-first-century metrics for student success" including "the knowledge, capabilities, and personal qualities . . . that will enable them to both thrive and contribute in a fast-changing economy and in turbulent, highly demanding global, societal, and often personal contexts" (Schneider, 2008, p. 2). These qualities are certainly equally important for community college students.

NEW DIRECTIONS FOR COMMUNITY COLLEGES • DOI: 10.1002/cc

In developing practice descriptions (particularly for programmatic interventions) and in identifying overlap and relationships between practices, we considered the following key features and dimensions: (a) purposes/goals, (b) activities and program components/structure, (c) timing/duration, (d) participants and role of institutional agents, (e) relevant contextual conditions, and (f) expected outcomes.

Purposes/Goals. According to Melguizo, Kienzl, and Kosiewicz (2013), the purpose of programs might be categorized as either academic preparation or providing information to students. For example, accelerated remediation, bridge programs, and supplemental instruction are practices most often designed to support students' academic preparation. At the same time, it is not uncommon for practices to be designed with multiple and/or overlapping purposes and goals. For instance, the purposes or goals of a learning community may include academic preparation and providing various forms of information to support students' transition to college.

Activities and Program Components/Structure. The typology of programmatic student success interventions proposed by Hatch and Bohlig (2016) suggests that "what distinguishes programs is not so much differences in their main purpose, but differences in the curricular and programmatic elements used to enact those purposes" (p. 22). For example, learning communities receive a lot of attention for their potential impact and typologies have been created to distinguish nuances among them. Yet, aside from their fundamental characteristic of linked courses, learning communities—at least in the community college setting—often share many of the same curricular features of other first-year seminars and student success courses. Similarly, the emerging trend of corequisite remediation in community colleges often links college-level courses with supplementary coursework or integrates tutoring and supplemental instruction. Arguably, this model is not unlike the design of learning communities more broadly.

Timing/Duration. It is notable that many recommended practices are typically provided as early college experiences. CCCSE (2012) characterized several practices as geared toward "planning" and "initiating" for success (p. 8), while recognizing that meaningful improvements to student outcomes require effective practices that are provided throughout students' experiences in college (Bailey & Smith Jaggars, 2015). We concur that several of the practices that prototypically happen early on (e.g., academic planning and goal setting) should be an ongoing process throughout students' experiences. Other practices such as early alert systems, tutoring, class attendance, and service learning have been developed to "sustain success" (CCCSE, 2012, p. 8). Additionally, a few practices such as research and capstone projects naturally occur later in a student's college experience. Among all practices discussed in this issue, the duration varies widely across instances and institutions according to local circumstances.

Participants and Role of Institutional Agents. Naturally, students are the primary participants of interest in programs and practices. Many practices, such as learning communities and orientation, are often specifically designed for targeted groups of students who are thought to require higher levels of support (Mellow & Heelan, 2008). Various practices often target certain groups of students including those from historically underrepresented and marginalized groups (Finley & McNair, 2013), those who place into developmental coursework, or students who enroll in targeted disciplines such as science, technology, engineering, and math (STEM), to name just a few.

Levin and colleagues (2010) assert that "program practices derive more from people than they do from policies, and promising practices derive especially from the adaptability of those involved with the program, including faculty members, staff members, and administrators" (p. 54). As such, we consider institutional agents to be an important feature in distinguishing and describing promising practices. Whereas some practices may, and often do, rely on a relatively well-defined team of staff, faculty, and administrators (in the case of orientation and first-year seminars, for instance), other practices, such as broad curricular features or practices we categorize as interventions, junctures, policies, and procedures, are typically decentralized and managed by faculty, staff, and administrators in the course of their regular work.

Relevant Contextual Conditions.   Young and Keup (Chapter 5) emphasize the importance of understanding the features of the educational environment that lead to improved educational outcomes for particular groups of students. Astin (1993) notes that, "in its broadest sense, the environment encompasses everything that happens to a student during the course of an educational program that might conceivably influence the outcomes under consideration. This includes not only the programs, personnel, curricula, teaching practices, and facilities that we consider to be part of any educational program but also the social and institutional climate in which the program operates" (p. 81). Unfortunately, the context or environment surrounding practices is too often not taken into consideration when adopting and adapting practices across contexts. Similarly, current research too often relies on single-institutions studies that limit the comparability of findings across studies (Crisp & Taggart, 2013). Although not well studied or documented, additional contextual conditions such as resources, concurrent practices/programs, connections with the local community, administrative support, and campus culture, among others may perhaps serve to meaningfully characterize practices on community college campuses (Haberler & Levin, 2014).

Expected Outcomes.   As previously mentioned, AAC&U High-Impact Practices, including undergraduate research, common intellectual experiences, and collaborative assignments, are largely centered around and designed to promote student engagement and learning outcomes. In contrast, CCCSE promising practices are predominantly focused on academic student success outcomes (both intermediary and longitudinal). For instance, interventions and policies, such as regular class attendance and early alert and intervention, are commonly designed to promote short-term academic outcomes such as within-term retention and class completion whereas other practices, such as goal setting and planning and first-year seminars, may be more focused toward longer-term outcomes (e.g., year-to-year retention and degree completion).

Describing and Mapping High-Impact and Promising Practices

We offer readers Figure 1.1 as one way to map recognized practices in terms of at least some of the five features just described. We do not necessarily offer this map as a conceptual framework but rather as a *heuristic* map—a visual tool for exploring a wide variety of practices and how their key features or dimensions may distinguish or connect them to each other. The vertical axis in Figure 1.1 represents how practices may be more or less "curricular" in nature and thus reflects an important aspect of a program's purposes and activities. We propose five rough categories of practices along this continuum that we tentatively call (a) programmatic interventions, (b) broad curricular features, (c) support services and ancillary instruction, (d) interventions and junctures, and (e) policies and procedures. In turn, Table 1.1 organizes our descriptions around these five groupings. The horizontal axis in Figure 1.1 reflects the timing/duration of practices, with practices mapped roughly to where they ideally, typically, or prototypically occur. Other features and dimensions of high-impact practices are not mapped but are noted in our descriptions.

Although not exhaustive, and certainly not meant to be mutually exclusive, this list of what may be called *promising* or—pending more evidence

Figure 1.1.   Heuristic Map of Proposed Promising and High-Impact Practices

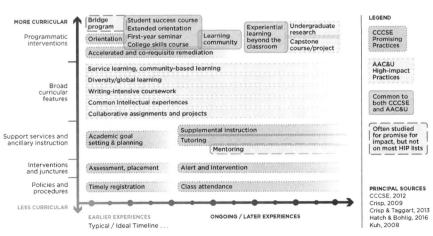

Table 1.1   Descriptions of High-Impact and Promising Practices

Programs and Practices	Description
Programmatic Interventions	
First-Year Seminars/Student Success Courses*,†	Designed to provide skills, knowledge, and support networks for successful college-going. Curriculum and structure vary but may include campus information, noncognitive skills, career exploration, and goal setting, among many other learning outcomes. Often tailored for students new to college or other at-risk populations (e.g., first-generation and developmental).
Learning Communities*,†	Designed to engage students in multiple ways and establish academic and social networks. Involves the coenrollment of a cohort of students into multiple courses that are integrated or linked. May include an integrated and interdisciplinary curriculum. The curriculum may share similarities with first-year seminars and student success courses. May or may not target particular groups of students.
Orientation†	Curriculum varies in length and content ranging from a single meeting for students new to an institution to a full-length credit-bearing course substantively equivalent to first-year seminars and student success courses.
Bridge Programs	Accelerated learning opportunities provided to students the summer prior to entering college. Use a variety of tutoring, workshops, and classroom instruction, including college skills and knowledge akin to orientation, first-year seminars, and student success courses.
Accelerated and Corequisite Remediation†	Policies and courses designed to move underprepared students into college-level math or English in an accelerated time frame and/or support these students to successfully complete these gateway courses. Formats vary from placement test preparation, self-paced modules, bundled developmental courses, developmental courses paired with college-level courses, or ancillary instruction.
Experiential Learning Beyond the Classroom (Including Internships)*,†	Experiential learning designed to provide students with practical work experiences.
Undergraduate Research*	Designed to engage students in the process of systematic empirical investigation. Most commonly used in science disciplines. In community colleges, increasingly offered in collaboration with 4-year universities.
Capstone Courses/Projects*	Summative experience required toward the end of an academic program that requires students to synthesize and apply what they have learned. May include a paper, portfolio, exhibit, or other assignment.

(Continued)

Table 1.1   Continued

Programs and Practices	Description
Broad Curricular Features	
Service Learning, Community-Based Learning*	Field-based experiential learning strategy that involves community service. Typically part of a formal course. Aimed at promoting self-reflection and civic engagement.
Diversity/Global Learning*	Class or program designed to assist students in exploring worldviews, perspectives, and cultures different from their own.
Writing-Intensive Coursework*	Coursework that emphasizes writing assignments/projects across the curriculum. Students write for various audiences in different disciplines.
Common Intellectual Experiences*	Shared curricular and cocurricular options for students that include participation in a set of required common courses or organized general education program. May center on broad themes, such as technology.
Collaborative Assignments and Projects*	Learning approach that teaches students to work together to solve problems and listen and learn from others. May involve activities, such as study groups, cooperative assignments, or team-based learning activities.
Support Services and Ancillary Instruction	
Goal Setting and Planning[†]	Advising experiences that guide students in setting academic goals and appropriate program plans, optimally in light of work, family, and other demands.
Supplemental Instruction[†]	A form of tutoring that involves a trained assistant (often a former student who successfully completed the course) providing academic support.
Tutoring[†]	Participation in required or voluntary tutoring services, as recipients and/or providers.
Mentoring[‡]	Students engage in relationships with mentors on and off-campus that provide various types of support, including academic and subject knowledge support, psychological and emotional support, degree and career support, and the presence of a role model.
Interventions and Junctures	
Assessment, Placement[†]	Placement preparation and exams to ascertain appropriate level of coursework.
Early Alert and Intervention[†]	Active or passive academic warning systems to identify students who need early support.
Policies and Procedures	
Timely Registration[†]	Requiring or encouraging students to enroll in courses prior to the first class meeting.
Class Attendance[†]	Attendance policies that encourage students to attend classes on a regular basis throughout the term.

*High-Impact Educational Practice identified by AAC&U.
[†]Promising Practice identified by CCCSE.
[‡]Forms of mentoring support proposed by Crisp.
[§]*Sources*: Bers & Younger, 2014; CCCSE, 2012; Cho & Karp, 2013; Crisp, 2009; Crisp & Taggart, 2013; Hatch & Bohlig, 2016; Jaggars, Hodara, Cho, & Xu, 2014; Karp, Raufman, Efthimiou, & Ritze, 2015; Kuh, 2008; Melguizo, Kienzl, & Kosiewicz, 2013; Mitchell, Alozie, & Wathington, 2015; Taggart & Crisp, 2011; Weiss et al., 2014.

in our view—*high-impact practices*, we hope these definitions offer for practitioners in particular an expansive view of practices to potentially adopt, adapt, and assess according to local needs. Instead of a list of distinct practices, we would offer that the idea of *high-impact practices* is an invitation to continue working to identify and verify which practices are indeed the best to which we can aspire and actually implement given practical limitations. Similarly, for researchers, the term *high-impact practices* proposes a hypothesis to be tested, a call to gather evidence to verify the claim of impact and to explore the experience of individuals and institutions in pursuing them.

References

Astin, A. (1993). *What matters in college: Four critical years revisited.* San Francisco, CA: Jossey-Bass.

Bailey, T. R., & Smith Jaggars, S. (2015). *Redesigning America's community colleges: A clearer path to student success.* Cambridge, MA: Harvard University Press.

Bers, T., & Younger, D. (2014). The first-year experience in community colleges. In R. D. Padgett (Ed.), *New Directions for Institutional Research: No. 160. Emerging research and practices on first-year students* (pp. 77–93). San Francisco, CA: Jossey-Bass.

Center for Community College Student Engagement. (2012). *A matter of degrees: Promising practices for community college student success (a first look).* Austin, TX: The University of Texas at Austin, Community College Leadership Program.

Cho, S-W., & Karp, M. M. (2013). Student success courses in the community college: Early enrollment and educational outcomes. *Community College Review, 41*(1), 86–103.

Crisp, G. (2009). Conceptualization and initial validation of the College Student Mentoring Scale (CSMS). *Journal of College Student Development, 50*(2), 177–194. doi:10.1353/csd.0.0061

Crisp, G. (2010). The impact of mentoring on community college students' intent to persist. *Review of Higher Education, 34*(1), 39–60. doi: 10.1353/rhe.2010.0003

Crisp, G., & Taggart, A. (2013). Community college student success programs: A synthesis, critique, and research agenda. *Community College Journal of Research and Practice, 37*(2), 114–130.

Finley, A., & McNair, T. (2013). *Assessing underserved students' engagement in high-impact practices.* Washington, DC: Association of American Colleges & Universities. Retrieved from http://www.aacu.org/assessinghips

Haberler, Z., & Levin, J. S. (2014). The four Cs of promising practices in community colleges. *Community College Journal of Research and Practice, 38*(5), 403–416. doi: 10.1080/10668926.2012.748381

Hatch, D. K., & Bohlig, E. M. (2016). An empirical typology of the latent programmatic structure of promising practices at community colleges. *Research in Higher Education, 57*(1), 72–98. doi:10.1007/s11162-015-9379-6

Jaggars, S. S., Hodara, M., Cho, S-W., & Xu, D. (2014). Three accelerated developmental education programs: Features, student outcomes and implications. *Community College Review, 43*(1), 3–26.

Jenkins, D., & Cho, S.-W. (2013). Get with the program … and finish it: Building guided pathways to accelerate student completion. In B. C. Phillips & J. E. Horowitz (Eds.), *New Directions for Community Colleges: No. 164. The college completion agenda: Practical approaches for reaching the big goal* (pp. 27–35). San Francisco, CA: Jossey-Bass. doi:10.1002/cc.20078

Karp, M. M., Raufman, J., Efthimiou, C., & Ritze, N. (2015). *Redesigning a student success course for sustained impact: Early outcomes findings* (CCRC Working Paper No. 81).

New York, NY: Columbia University, Teachers College, Community College Research Center.

Kuh, G. D. (2008). *High-impact educational practices: What they are, who has access to them, and why they matter*. Washington, DC: Association of American Colleges & Universities.

Levin, J. S., Cox, E. M., Cerven, C., & Haberler, Z. (2010). The recipe for promising practices in community colleges. *Community College Review, 38*(1), 31–58.

Melguizo, T., Kienzl, G., & Kosiewicz, H. (2013). The potential of community colleges to increase bachelor's degree attainment rates. In L. W. Perna & A. P. Jones (Eds.), *The state of college access and completion* (pp. 115–139). New York, NY: Routledge.

Mellow, G. O., & Heelan, C. (2008). *Minding the dream: The process and practice of the American community college*. Lanham, MD: Roman & Littlefield.

Mitchell, C. E., Alozie, N. M., & Wathington, H. D. (2015). Investigating the potential of community college developmental summer bridge programs in facilitating student adjustment to four-year institutions. *Community College Journal of Research and Practice, 39*(4), 366–382. doi:10.1080/10668926.2014.981891

Schneider, C. G. (2008). Introduction: Liberal education and high-impact practices: Making excellence-once and for all-inclusive. In G. D. Kuh (Ed.), *High-impact educational practices: What they are, who has access to, and why they matter* (pp. 1–8). Washington, DC: Association of American Colleges & Universities.

Taggart, A., & Crisp, G. (2011). A synthesis and critique of service learning at community colleges. *Journal of College Reading and Learning, 42*(1), 24–39.

Weiss, M. J., Mayer, A. K., Cullinan, D., Ratledge, A., Sommo, C., & Diamond, J. (2014). *A random assignment evaluation of learning communities at Kingsborough Community College: Seven years later*. New York, NY: MDRC.

DERYL K. HATCH *is assistant professor of educational administration at the University of Nebraska–Lincoln.*

GLORIA CRISP *is an associate professor, College of Education, Oregon State University at Corvallis, Oregon.*

KATHERINE WESLEY *is assistant professor of practice at the University of Nebraska–Lincoln, and executive director, National Council of Instructional Administrators.*

NEW DIRECTIONS FOR COMMUNITY COLLEGES • DOI: 10.1002/cc

2

This chapter reviews ways that researchers have presented variously narrow and broad groupings of special student success programs over the course of decades. Cultural Historical Activity Theory (CHAT) is proposed as a way to conceptualize various kinds of community college student success programs as instances of a more general type of program.

A Brief History and a Framework for Understanding Commonalities and Differences of Community College Student Success Programs

Deryl K. Hatch

There is today broad consensus among policy makers and higher education stakeholders that community colleges are key to achieving goals to increase the portion of adults with postsecondary credentials. In turn, community colleges educators look to new or innovative pedagogical and institutional structures to realize these goals. Key among efforts to enhance student success are a select few policies and practices singled out as holding particular promise to move the needle on community college persistence and completion. Such *promising* and *high-impact practices* (HIPs) include first-year seminars, student skills courses, college success strategies courses, extended orientation programs, and many others described throughout this issue. Though long used and studied, they have received renewed attention (see recent literature reviews by Bailey & Alfonso, 2005; Brownell & Swaner, 2009a; Crisp & Taggart, 2013; Swaner & Brownell, 2009).

A substantial challenge to this renewed effort to identify high-impact practices is in fact the perennial quandary of how to define them and circumscribe a set of them. Arguably, good practices for undergraduate education are not novel (Chickering & Gamson, 1987), only underused. But is there more to what conceptually defines and links them beyond their purported benefits? If we are to seek better evidence of their effectiveness and ways to scale them up, it follows that a first step is to establish what "they" are in the first place. My purpose in this chapter is, first, to explore the

NEW DIRECTIONS FOR COMMUNITY COLLEGES, no. 175, Fall 2016 © 2016 Wiley Periodicals, Inc.
Published online in Wiley Online Library (wileyonlinelibrary.com) • DOI: 10.1002/cc.20209

history of how authors have identified and grouped special student success programs for the community college setting and, second, to propose the use of cultural historical activity theory (CHAT; Engeström, 1993; Leont'ev, 1978; Vygotsky, 1987) as a way to conceptualize certain related types of student success programs as instances of a more general type of intervention in a way that can inform the work of researchers and practitioners.

A History of Ad Hoc Groupings of Special and High-Impact Practices

Certain college student success courses, programs, and interventions have long received attention as exemplary or distinctive practices for promoting students' successful transition to college and their acquisition of college knowledge, skills, and support networks. What has varied is which practices have been called out as special. Kulik, Kulik, and Shwalb (1983) reviewed the evidence in the literature from the 1930s to the1970s regarding the effectiveness of what they termed *special programs for high-risk students* on outcomes of achievement (grades) and persistence. They characterized certain programs according to the decades in which they appeared and, in their view, as a function of the broadening inclusion of historically underrepresented and underserved[1] groups in higher education through the emergence of the civil rights movements. These special programs were *reading and learning skills courses* (1930s and 1940s); *group-oriented guidance sessions* (1950s and 1960s); and *comprehensive support programs* (late 1960s) that combined tutoring, advising, learning centers, skills courses, and other services.

In the mid-1990s, the National Resource Center for The First-Year Experience and Students in Transition published a volume of essays (Hankin, 1996) regarding a broad range of programs, practices, and some policy issues related to "opportunity and access" for first-year students in the community college sector. In the first chapter, Hankin and Gardner (1996) recommended the implementation of multiple "mechanisms" (p. 10) from *mentoring* and *advising*, to *freshman seminars* (what they would today call first-year seminars), to *tutoring*, to *early-warning procedures*, among many other programmatic and institutional structures, all of which are understood as responding to the heterogeneity of students and their needs. Thus, in their view, no list per se of impactful practices exists. Instead, they present the notion of The First-Year Experience as an expansive, comprehensive philosophy that engenders a "deliberately designed attempt to provide a rite of passage in which the students are supported, welcomed, celebrated, and ultimately assimilated" (p. 10).

Ten years later, Bailey and Alfonso (2005) presented a review of evidence regarding the effectiveness of practices to increase persistence and completion specific to the community college sector. They included three groupings for various practices: (a) *advising, counseling, mentoring,* and *orientation programs*; (b) *learning communities*; and (c) *developmental educa-tion*. They also included the general idea of college-wide *institutional reform* as an effective practice for community colleges.

Also in the 2000s, Swaner and Brownell (2009; see also Brownell & Swaner, 2009a, 2009b) reviewed the literature regarding evidence for the effectiveness of HIPs for traditionally underserved student populations by considering dozens of outcomes. They limited their review to *learning com-munities, service learning, undergraduate research, first-year seminars*, and *capstone courses and projects*, which are only 5 of 10 HIPs identified by the Association of American Colleges and Universities (AAC&U, 2007), which commissioned the study (see also Finley & McNair, 2013; Kuh, 2008; Kuh & O'Donnell, 2013).

In a series of three reports, the Center for Community College Student Engagement (CCCSE, 2012, 2013, 2014) investigated 13 of what they called *promising practices* (PPs) for the community college sector, spanning a wide range of interventions, including programmatic offerings, policies, and pro-cedures. Notably, both CCCSE's and AAC&U's work in this area stems from an interrelated body of engagement research based on data from the Com-munity College Survey of Student Engagement (CCSSE) and the National Survey of Student Engagement (NSSE); yet, CCCSE's PPs and AAC&U's HIPs overlap in just two areas: *experiential learning beyond the classroom* (including internships) and student success programs, such as *first-year seminars* and *learning communities*. This divergence may well reflect the dif-fering values and missions of the 4-year vs. 2-year college sector, or that of the organizations that produced the reports, or both.

More recently, Crisp and Taggart (2013) in their literature review on student success programs at community colleges, selected *learning com-munities, student success courses*, and *supplemental instruction* from among "numerous programmatic efforts" based on the straightforward rationale that they are "three of the most prominent programmatic efforts currently implemented at community colleges" .... designed "to provide students with opportunities to become socially and academically integrated into the college environment, connect with faculty and staff at the college, and/or overcome a potential lack of cultural capital or academic preparedness" (pp. 115,118).

Across all of these literature reviews and reports, and reflective of many individual studies they include, authors repeatedly rely on the rationale of the preponderance of research studies to define the scope or list of which practices hold particular promise of high impact. As a result, different lists include different programs, policies, and add-on features. CCCSE's (2012, 2013, 2014) list is thus far the most expansive inventory of special com-munity college student success practices in the literature. It is also arguably the only one to offer a conceptual categorization of practices, even if tenta-tive: the first of the CCCSE's three reports in this series grouped practices according to their primary function of either *planning for success, initiating success*, or *sustaining success*. Using this scheme, Table 2.1 summarizes various groupings and categories that authors have used over the years.

Limitations Due to a Lack of Conceptualizations of HIPs

Having various lists of promising practices for higher education is certainly not problematic on its own. But the use of the *high-impact* label in the absence of criterion-based or conceptual definitions may tend to give existing labels undue importance, potentially stifling innovation, and broader implementation of programs or the mechanisms that make them work (Kuh et al., 2013). For instance, it can be argued that high-impact or promising practices are ultimately manifestations of, or thoughtfully crafted vehicles for, general principles of good educational practice (Chickering & Gamson, 1987), which in turn are ultimately related to the central questions of effective learning and teaching that have been debated and researched for centuries. In this view, a list of HIPs may be unnecessarily reductive.

Indeed, Karp (Chapter 3) advocates that a principle-driven consideration of student success interventions is needed rather than the predominant program-driven view. Karp argues that there are *processes* or *mechanisms* of nonacademic student support that can be integrated within formal programmatic structures and informally or organically throughout college, especially classrooms. However, Karp encountered a fundamental challenge in undertaking her review that illustrates the need for a coherent conceptualization of the very HIPs she turned to in deriving mechanisms of student support. Namely,

> the myriad approaches to providing non-academic support result in the inclusion of many different programs in this body of literature.... Moreover, evaluations of nonacademic supports tend to group different interventions under the same category. For example, the "learning community" literature incorporates a range of programs that include multiple and widely varying components. As a result, it is not always possible to isolate the effects of a specific program element. (Karp, 2011, p. 4)

Thus, whether the task is to derive principles/processes/mechanisms of effective practice by unpacking promising interventions, or conversely to identify promising interventions based on their use of effective principles/processes/mechanisms, the challenge is conceptual and in fact twofold. To define a practice as high impact, we must measure its effectiveness, yet to measure its effectiveness, we must conceptually define *it* in the first place. I argue that in the absence of a satisfactory conceptualization of HIPs with which to bridge this circular problem, there is a limit to the ability to derive generalizable principles of program design and impact that researchers have called for (Bailey & Alfonso, 2005; Crisp & Taggart, 2013; Hatch, 2012; Swaner & Brownell, 2009).

Table 2.1 Special, Promising, and High-Impact Practices Named in Selected Literature Reviews and Institutional Reports

Categories and Principal Timing of Interventions as Proposed by CCCSE (2012)

	Planning for Success			Initiating Success			Sustaining Success					Others*
	Assessment and Placement	Timely Registration	Academic Advising	Orientation, First-Year Seminars, College Success Courses	Learning Communities	Accelerated Developmental Education	Early Warning Programs	Experiential Learning, Internships	Tutoring	Supplemental Instruction	Class Attendance (and Policies)	Collaborative Learning Practices
Kulik, Kulik, & Shwalb (1983)			X	X		X						
Hankin (1996)*	X	X	X	X	X	X	X		X	X		X
Bailey & Alfonso (2005)			X	X	X	X						
AAC&U (2007; cf. Swaner & Brownell, 2009)*				X	X							X
Karp (2011)			X	X	X							
CCCSE (2012, 2013, 2014)	X	X	X	X	X	X	X	X	X	X	X	
Crisp & Taggart (2013)				X	X					X		

*Hankin (1996) includes programs noted in this table plus policy considerations that are understood as forming a comprehensive "First-Year Experience" philosophy.

Conceptualizing Structured Student Success Programs as Activity Systems

Despite the lack of conceptual definitions for HIPs, some programs seem to fit together intuitively. CCCSE's (2012) tentative framework identifies five programs in particular that are more frequently studied among other high-impact practices and often grouped together (see Table 2.1): first-year seminars, college success courses, learning communities, orientation programs, and accelerated developmental education. CCCSE referred to these interventions as "structured group learning experiences" (SGLEs) and noted that they "reflect the goal of ensuring that students are successful in the early weeks and then through the first year of college [though] they can occur at different points in students' entering experiences and extend over differing time periods" (CCCSE, 2012, p. 16). Evidence shows that indeed they often have as much in common as what differentiates them in curricular features (Hatch & Bohlig, 2016).

I propose that cultural historical activity theory (CHAT) offers a compelling framework for explaining why these programs resemble one another and form a common group, not just in a general conceptual way but in terms that provide specific ways for researchers and practitioners to understand and unpack their complex structures. The key is in how CHAT views human interactions as driven by goals within a culturally bound system of individuals who, collectively, use tools and artifacts to accomplish those goals in light of rules and cultural norms. This is what is called sociocultural activity, and it can be effective and harmonious or inefficient and riddled with inherent tensions. The goal of CHAT is largely to uncover inherent tensions to improve practice.

CHAT, sometimes termed just activity theory, traces its history to the work of Russian educational psychologist Lev Vygotsky and colleagues (Roth & Lee, 2007; Vygotsky, 1987). Vygotsky proposed that classical ideas suggesting that human behavior is a function of stimulus and response were too simplistic to explain real-world, complicated human interactions. His innovation was to propose that tools, both concrete and abstract, mediate the relationship between individuals and their actions. Accordingly, humans continually forge new tools and social artifacts to navigate their collective and individual goals. This three-way relationship forms the basic structure of an activity system (Engeström, 2000, 2010). An activity system consists of its *participants*, the *object* or motive of the activity, its mediating *artifacts* (instruments, tools, symbols, and prior knowledge), the *rules* generally followed in carrying out the activity, the *community* of peers or colleagues involved in the activity, and the *division of labor* within the activity.

The outcome of an activity system—that is, the work produced or, in this case, desired student outcomes of persistence, graduation, transfer, among others—is external to the system itself. But the object (also called the purpose, motive, the immediate task) that people work on together to

NEW DIRECTIONS FOR COMMUNITY COLLEGES • DOI: 10.1002/cc

ultimately achieve that outcome is a defining aspect of the system. This distinction between goals and outcomes has parallels in the field of program evaluation (see McComb and Lyddon, Chapter 7). In my reading of the research literature, and reflected in the literature reviews (Bailey & Alfonso, 2005; CCCSE, 2012; Crisp & Taggart, 2013; Hankin & Gardner, 1996; Kulik et al., 1983; Swaner & Brownell, 2009), I find that authors consistently characterize student success programs and interventions—despite their particulars—as ultimately designed around a common set of purposes: to socialize entering students to college life and equip them with the self-regulatory skills, knowledge, and social and academic networks that are associated with later positive outcomes.

CHAT posits that "the main thing that distinguishes one activity from another . . . is the difference between their objects [which] gives [them] a determined direction . . . the object of the activity is its true motive" (Leont'ev, 1978, p. 62). The object is "the reason why individuals and groups choose to participate in an activity . . . and what holds together the elements of an activity . . . [and] may lead them to create or gain new artifacts or cultural tools intended to make the activity robust" (Yamagata-Lynch, 2010, p. 17). In this view, CHAT suggests that student success courses and programs, in all their variations, may be instances of a broader kind of activity and explains why they are intuitively connected. I call this concept a structured group socialization experience (SGSE), a term adapted from CCCSE's label, structured group learning experiences (SGLEs; CCCSE, 2012), in recognition of their sociocultural nature that links them.

Using Activity Theory in Research and Practice of Student Success Programs

CHAT as applied to student success programs is as relevant to practice as to research. The implications of this framework for both are presented below. For a more in-depth treatment of CHAT in educational research and practice, I refer readers to Roth and Lee's (2007) article in *Review of Educational Research* and to Yamagata-Lynch's (2010) book, which describes in practical terms how to undertake activity system analysis, one of the methodological approaches to CHAT research.

Implications for Practice.   CHAT is not just a useful theoretical notion. Just as important, CHAT provides a framework for practitioners to understand and improve their practice. In fact, CHAT was originally created not necessarily for scholarly investigation, but as a way for practitioners themselves to reflect on their own day-to-day work and improve systems to better achieve desired outcomes (Engeström, 1993). CHAT takes a systemic view of daily work to unpack how individuals work together toward goals and to find ways to improve that collaboration. CHAT recognizes that human systems of work are inherently characterized by inner contradictions, and so the goal of applying CHAT to understand work processes is to uncover those contradictions and find resolutions to them (through the clarification of goals, the creation of new tools, new rules, or the involvement of people in new ways, among other ways). This process, like any institutional improvement or change, can be haphazard or it can be purposeful. CHAT provides practitioners with a way to understand their work and a process to make it better. That is to say, CHAT is much more than a way understand *practice* in abstract terms. Rather, it calls for engaging in what some refer to as *praxis*, which is applying and enacting an ongoing process of learning and growing (Grundy, 1987). In short, this is a type of institutional reform that Bailey and Alfonso (2005) called for to improve community college persistence.

Roth and Lee (2007) reviewed some of the most prominent examples of how CHAT has been used in this practical manner. Primary among them are the *change laboratory* (Engeström, Virkkunen, Helle, Pihlaja, & Poikela, 1996) and *boundary-crossing laboratory* (Engeström, 2010). In a change laboratory, a work group is convened that involves all stakeholders in the program, from administrators to faculty to students. The work group uses a rich set of tools (video recordings, databases, editing software, etc.) for collectively identifying tensions that occur in a system in order to develop new work processes that overcome these tensions. A boundary-crossing laboratory extends this idea to work accomplished by multiple groups or across systems, such as academic divisions or between, say, academic affairs and student services. These laboratories share similarities with systems theory (Senge, 2006) and other popular quality improvement processes (Dew & Nearing, 2004) but go beyond the goal of *managing* institutional function to being the purview of workers *conducting* the work themselves.

Possibilities for these laboratories as applied to community college student success programs are illustrated in two studies (Engeström, Engeström, & Suntio, 2002a, 2002b) that describe change laboratories convened by middle-school faculty members to establish a new vision for the school and devise practices to achieve the vision. The goal to align practice with vision is common to nearly all educational settings, including community colleges. Similar to many community colleges and the students they serve, the case described by Engeström and colleagues was of an institution situated in an economically disadvantaged area with a large population of recent immigrants and refugees. To accomplish their task of aligning practice with their vision, faculty members and researchers came together in weekly 2-hour sessions over the course of 11 weeks to analyze their daily work, unpack assumptions of their actions, and devise new curricular and pedagogical goals. Researchers tracked the implementation of their proposed innovations over the subsequent 18 months to observe what practitioners did to improve their own work.

During the change laboratories, faculty members used the dimensions of activity systems to describe how things currently operate and how things would best operate. In this way, they tracked the roots of classroom tensions, which at first instructors characterized as problems arising from student poverty, apathy, and lack of preparation. But by considering a systemic understanding of the individual, social, and institutional settings of their practice, faculty members converged on the concept of a capstone project that was personally meaningful to students and represented something more than just a final report card—something the students could take pride in and show to family and school officials. In the course of devising this new curricular goal, the researchers observed that instructors' manner of speaking about their students turned from predominantly negative attributes of apathy and incompetency (clearly deficit-oriented perspectives) to predominantly positive attributes of their energy and competency. The change was gradual and came about only in relation to how they themselves understood the entire system collectively.

Rather than just a curricular innovation, the change laboratories spurred an institutional innovation by working through everyday tasks that needed to be accomplished. This is an example of organically developing and implementing one kind of high-impact practice—in this case, a capstone project—through critical self-examination of practices by practitioners, rather than as a token practice implemented in a silo or by an independent group. The researchers attributed the faculty members' success in improving their work to their being attentive to the *multiple voices* of many participants who collectively constitute the activity system of diverse classrooms where the school was situated.

This last idea relates to other applications that Roth and Lee (2007) recommend to practitioners of a *coteaching/cogenerative dialoguing* model wherein coteaching by all stakeholders informs curriculum redesign. Cogenerative dialoguing occurs as "all participants contribute to the emerging understanding and theories of practice, and a checklist is elaborated to monitor these sessions so that individual voices are not silenced" (Roth & Lee, 2007, p. 212), including the voices of the students themselves (Bondi, 2013). This approach has the potential to accomplish fundamental changes in how we collectively make sense of how students, especially the most vulnerable cultural communities in the United States, engage in collegegoing (Gildersleeve, 2010). This approach to improving educational practices more readily leads educators to using an asset-based approach that creates spaces for the critical voices of students and puts the burden on the system and institution broadly, instead of common deficit-based approaches that put the burden on marginalized students to make improvements (see Acevedo-Gil & Zerquera, Chapter 6).

Implications for Research.   CHAT is traditionally used in qualitative studies and readily lends itself to methodically documenting and analyzing complex human interactions as they develop over time (Roth & Lee, 2007). The added value that CHAT and related analyses bring to qualitative research includes its ability to simultaneously account for multiple layers of real-world human experiences while contextualizing them within the whole. The unit of analysis is human activity itself, embedded within its so-cial context. The result is the ability to unpack both instances and patterns of why and how systems work, not just the themes or principles that char-acterize them. The level of analysis is scalable from particular episodes of interactions to programs to whole institutions.

Though rare, quantitative analyses using CHAT as a framework have proven useful where the object is to understand differences in outcomes resulting from program heterogeneity, rather than differences attributable merely to the dichotomous measure of participation or nonparticipation (Atteberry & Bryk, 2011; Plewis & Mason, 2005). In a quantitative study, this means operationalizing multiple levels of variables within a single ana-lytical model and then interpreting the findings in light of the whole, prefer-ably using a longitudinal research design to account for how the influence of system elements may change over time.

CHAT can be used to address many of the shortcomings of the research literature on HIPs. Some instances follow. Kulik and colleagues (1983) found that newly implemented special programs are more effective than in-stitutionalized programs. They hypothesized that this was related mostly to a dropoff in institutional energy, enthusiasm, and possibly funding for older programs, rather than inherent differences between program designs. CHAT is ideally suited to explore this hypothesis—not just whether such a dropoff occurs but if so how and why. According to Bailey and Alfonso (2005), an important limitation is that most studies on program effectiveness are based on single-institution samples, limiting the generalizability of findings. But by conceptualizing multiple programs across institutions as parallel types of activity systems, which necessarily account for local circumstances, CHAT helps address this problem. In another example, Crisp and Taggart (2013) "challenge researchers to be mindful of designing interventions that expose the participants to more than one treatment (e.g., simultaneous participa-tion in a learning community and mentoring program)...[so as to] avoid the threat of multiple treatment interference" (p. 126). Fidelity of program implementation is indeed too often a weak point in program effectiveness research, and there are techniques to limiting and therefore accounting for sources of variation in program effects (Weiss, Bloom, & Brock, 2013). But ultimately, extending the scope of program effectiveness research not just across multiple institutions but across related strands of literature requires us to flip the common and costly method of controlling implementation details to that of measuring the effects of a program in terms of variations in their implementation details. CHAT provides a framework to understand variations in programs designed for similar purposes, across research sites, and even across particular analytical methods.

Student Success Programs Among Many HIPs.   Last, and in broad terms, CHAT can inform the practice of SGSEs within a broader First-Year Experience (FYE), as envisioned by Hankin and Gardner (1996), who affirm that the FYE philosophy involves a notion of "intentionality" and "includes making a systematic study and effort to identify the variables that interfere with freshman success and then designing programs to address these variables" (p. 10). These ideas are reminiscent of the object-oriented nature of activity systems and the process of uncovering tensions and contradictions within them. Thus, an FYE can be thought of as a broad-reaching activity system made of multiple subsystems. The closer they are aligned around a common and central goal to ensure student success, with tools and rules and regulations and the division of labor aligned around that purpose, ostensibly the more likely tensions will be minimized or manageable. But systems outside of college—such as work, family, and transportation systems—often work at odds with the object of successful college-going. This suggests at least one possible reason for findings that programmatic impacts are limited or fade over time (Rutschow, Cullinan, & Welbeck, 2012). As students exit an SGSE, their integration in a larger community of practice that collectively pursues a common object may weaken as these other systems overwhelm their college success. If so, this would underscore the potential impact of both programmatic and diffused student success strategies that many have called for (CCCSE, 2012; Karp, Chapter 3) and that extend well beyond the first year (Nora, Barlow, & Crisp, 2005).

Whether student success programs and other high-impact practices are conceptualized in the terms I have proposed here or in other ways useful for their design, evaluation, and broader implementation (where the evidence actually turns out to be favorable), it is clear from current research and practice that a more coherent framework is needed than the current state of the art provides. Activity theory shows one way forward in conceptualizing, enacting, and evaluating a FYE philosophy of interlocking systems of activity of distributed promising practices.

Note

1. The terms Kulik, Kulik, and Shwalb (1983) used were "socially, economically, and educationally deprived groups . . . disadvantaged students" (p. 398). I opt to use the converse of these deficit-oriented terms.

References

Association of American Colleges & Universities. (2007). *College learning for the new global century: A report from the National Leadership Council for Liberal Education & America's Promise*. Washington, DC: Author.

Atteberry, A., & Bryk, A. S. (2011). Analyzing teacher participation in literacy coaching activities. *Elementary School Journal, 112*(2), 356–382.

Bailey, T., & Alfonso, M. (2005). *Paths to persistence: An analysis of research on program effectiveness at community colleges*. Indianapolis, IN: Lumina Foundation.

Bondi, S. (2013). Using cogenerative dialogues to improve teaching and learning. *About Campus, 18*(3), 2–8.

Brownell, J. E., & Swaner, L. E. (2009a). High-impact practices: Applying the learning outcomes literature to the development of successful campus programs. *Peer Review*, 11(2), 26–30.

Brownell, J. E., & Swaner, L. E. (2009b). Outcomes of high impact educational practices: A review of the literature. *Diversity & Democracy*, 12(2), 4–6.

Center for Community College Student Engagement. (2012). *A matter of degrees: Promising practices for community college student success (a first look)*. Austin, TX: The University of Texas at Austin, Community College Leadership Program.

Center for Community College Student Engagement. (2013). *A matter of degrees: Engaging practices, engaging students (high-impact practices for community college student engagement)*. Austin, TX: The University of Texas at Austin, Community College Leadership Program.

Center for Community College Student Engagement. (2014). *A matter of degrees: Practices to pathways (high-impact practices for community college student success)*. Austin, TX: The University of Texas at Austin, Community College Leadership Program.

Chickering, A. W., & Gamson, Z. F. (1987). Seven principles for good practice in undergraduate education. *AAHE Bulletin*, 39(7), 3–7.

Crisp, G., & Taggart, A. (2013). Community college student success programs: A synthesis, critique, and research agenda. *Community College Journal of Research and Practice*, 37(2), 114–130.

Dew, J. R., & Nearing, M. M. (2004). *Continuous quality improvement in higher education*. Westport, CT: Rowman & Littlefield.

Engeström, Y. (1993). Developmental studies of work as a testbench of activity theory: The case of primary care medical practice. In S. Chaiklin & J. Lave (Eds.), *Understanding practice: Perspectives on activity and context* (pp. 64–103). Cambridge, United Kingdom: Cambridge University Press.

Engeström, Y. (2000). Activity theory as a framework for analyzing and redesigning work. *Ergonomics*, 43(7), 960–974.

Engeström, Y. (2010). Expansive learning at work: Toward an activity theoretical reconceptualization. *Journal of Education and Work*, 14(1), 133–156.

Engeström, Y., Engeström, R., & Suntio, A. (2002a). Can a school community learn to master its own future? An activity-theoretical study of expansive learning among middle school teachers. In G. Stahl (Ed.), *Computer support for collaborative learning: Foundations* (pp. 318–324). Mahwah, NJ: Lawrence Erlbaum.

Engeström, Y., Engeström, R., & Suntio, A. (2002b). Can a school community learn to master its own future? An activity-theoretical study of expansive learning among middle school teachers. In G. Wells & G. Claxton (Eds.), *Learning for life in the 21st century: Sociocultural perspectives on the future of education* (pp. 211–224). Oxford, United Kingdom: Blackwell.

Engeström, Y., Virkkunen, J., Helle, M., Pihlaja, J., & Poikela, R. (1996). The Change Laboratory as a tool for transforming work. *Lifelong Learning in Europe*, 1(2), 10–17.

Finley, A., & McNair, T. B. (2013). *Assessing underserved students' engagement in high-impact practices*. Washington, DC: Association of American Colleges & Universities.

Gildersleeve, R. E. (2010). *Fracturing opportunity: Mexican migrant students and college-going literacy* (2nd ed.). New York, NY: Peter Lang.

Grundy, S. (1987). *Curriculum: Product or praxis*. New York, NY: Routledge.

Hankin, J. N. (1996). *The community college: Opportunity and access for America's first-year students* (Monograph No. 19). Columbia, SC: University of South Carolina, National Resource Center for The First-Year Experience and Students in Transition.

Hankin, J. N., & Gardner, J. N. (1996). The freshman year experience: A philosophy for higher education in the new millennium. In J. N. Hankin (Ed.), *The community college: Opportunity and access for America's first-year students* (Monograph No. 19, pp. 1–10). Columbia, SC: University of South Carolina, National Resource Center for The First-Year Experience and Students in Transition.

Hatch, D. K. (2012). Unpacking the black box of student engagement: The need for programmatic investigation of high-impact practices. *Community College Journal of Research and Practice, 36*(11), 903–915.

Hatch, D. K., & Bohlig, E. M. (2016). An empirical typology of the latent programmatic structure of promising practices at community colleges. *Research in Higher Education, 57*(1), 72–98. doi:10.1007/s11162-015-9379-6

Karp, M. M. (2011). *Toward a new understanding of non-academic student support: Four mechanisms encouraging positive student outcomes in the community college* (CCRC Working Paper No. 28). New York, NY: Columbia University, Teachers College, Community College Research Center.

Kuh, G. D. (2008). *High-impact educational practices: What they are, who has access to them, and why they matter.* Washington, DC: Association of American Colleges & Universities.

Kuh, G. D., Hatch, D. K., Seifert, T. A., Finley, A., McNair, T. B., & Mayhew, M. J. (2013, November). *Data, methods, and evidence to identify high-impact practices.* Symposium presented at the annual meeting of the Association for the Study of Higher Education (ASHE), St. Louis, MO.

Kuh, G. D., & O'Donnell, K. (2013). *Ensuring quality & taking high-impact practices to scale.* Washington, DC: Association of American Colleges & Universities.

Kulik, C.-L. C., Kulik, J. A., & Shwalb, B. J. (1983). College programs for high-risk and disadvantaged students: A meta-analysis of findings. *Review of Educational Research, 53*(3), 397–414.

Leont'ev, A. N. (1978). *Activity, consciousness, and personality.* Englewood Cliffs, NJ: Prentice Hall.

Nora, A., Barlow, E., & Crisp, G. (2005). Student persistence and degree attainment beyond the first year in college. In A. Seidman (Ed.), *College retention: Formula for student success* (pp. 129–153). Westport, CT: ACE/Praeger.

Plewis, I., & Mason, P. (2005). What works and why: Combining quantitative and qualitative approaches in large-scale evaluations. *International Journal of Social Research Methodology, 8*(3), 185–194.

Roth, W.-M., & Lee, Y.-J. (2007). "Vygotsky's neglected legacy": Cultural-historical activity theory. *Review of Educational Research, 77*(2), 186–232.

Rutschow, E. Z., Cullinan, D., & Welbeck, R. (2012). *Keeping students on course: An impact study of a student success course at Guilford Technical Community College.* New York, NY: MDRC.

Senge, P. M. (2006). *The fifth discipline: The art and practice of the learning organization.* Westminster, MD: Random House.

Swaner, L. E., & Brownell, J. E. (2009). *Outcomes of high impact practices for underserved students: A review of the literature.* Prepared for the Association of American Colleges and Universities Project USA. Retrieved from http://www.heritage.edu/Portals/0/pdfs/Faculty_and_Staff/CILT/Outcomes_of_High_Impact_Practices.pdf

Vygotsky, L. S. (1987). *The collected works of L. S. Vygotsky* (R. W. Rieber & A. S. Carton, Eds.). New York, NY: Plenum.

Weiss, M. J., Bloom, H. S., & Brock, T. (2013). *A conceptual framework for studying the sources of variation in program effects.* New York, NY: MDRC.

Yamagata-Lynch, L. C. (2010). *Activity systems analysis methods: Understanding complex learning environments.* New York, NY: Springer.

DERYL K. HATCH *is an assistant professor of educational administration at the University of Nebraska–Lincoln.*

3

Despite their best efforts, community colleges continue to see low rates of student persistence and degree attainment. Although such outcomes can be attributed in large part to students' lack of academic readiness, nonacademic issues also play a part. Building on Karp's 2011 framework of nonacademic support, this chapter explores the evidence that holistic support can encourage community college students' success.

A Holistic Conception of Nonacademic Support: How Four Mechanisms Combine to Encourage Positive Student Outcomes in the Community College

Melinda Mechur Karp

Community college success depends not only upon students' academic skills but also on a set of nonacademic skills and behaviors (Karp & Bork, 2014). Colleges therefore implement an array of "nonacademic" support programs and practices to help students persist in postsecondary education and complete a credential. Such activities take myriad approaches; common programs include student success courses, enhanced or intrusive advising, and learning communities, among others. However, nonacademic support interventions, even when labelled the same thing, can differ substantially; for example, the "learning community" terminology incorporates a range of programs that include multiple and widely varying components.

A close read of the literature on nonacademic supports reveals that the specific service or program by which a support is delivered is less important than the underlying processes that encourage positive outcomes to occur. This chapter examines those underlying mechanisms. I update and extend my 2011 conception of nonacademic support in order to emphasize the need for holistic and multifaceted support services in the community college setting. Engaging in this update is particularly important given the surge of attention paid in recent years to helping students develop "noncognitive" skills thought to be related to academic success (see, for example, Farrington et al., 2012). Nonacademic support interventions often seek to

New Directions for Community Colleges, no. 175, Fall 2016 © 2016 Wiley Periodicals, Inc.
Published online in Wiley Online Library (wileyonlinelibrary.com) • DOI: 10.1002/cc.20210

develop noncognitive skills, which include constructs, such as mindsets, learning strategies, and social skills.

Identification of Four Nonacademic Support Mechanisms

In 2009 and 2010, several Community College Research Center (CCRC) colleagues and I engaged in an extensive review of the literature, examining persistence among academically vulnerable students at commuter and 2-year institutions. We defined "academically vulnerable" students as those from backgrounds that are correlated with low levels of postsecondary success, including those who are academically underprepared, from underrepresented minority groups, of low socioeconomic status, or having low levels of parental education. Our review focused on services, interventions, and informal activities that help students address the social, cultural, and otherwise implicit demands of college. We read and reviewed 128 books, journal articles, and reports. These included evaluations of common interventions and the most commonly cited theoretical works (including Tinto's [1993], Pascarella and Terenzini's [2005], and Braxton, Sullivan, & Johnson's [1997] seminal works in this area).

We initially sought to examine the evidence supporting specific types of interventions but found that the many approaches to providing nonacademic support made this approach difficult; recent research confirms the similarities among interventions (Hatch & Bohlig, 2016). For example, two programs may have the same title ("enhanced advising") but actually offer different types of services. Two other programs may be called by different names but offer the same type of support ("first-year seminars" and "orientations" emphasizing time management and study skills).

Therefore, we focused on the *type* of support offered, seeking underlying commonalities of the various interventions. We carefully analyzed the program description included in each study to inductively identify the main components of the intervention under investigation. Studies were grouped based on their common components. Through this process, we identified four key *mechanisms*, or the "things that happen" within programs and activities, encouraging positive student outcomes (Karp, 2011). To update the framework, in the summer of 2015, I conducted another literature review to find evaluations published in the past 5 years. In this chapter, I report on these new studies within each mechanism described below.

Creating Social Relationships.   Developing social relationships is important to student success for two reasons. First, they appear to help students become connected to college. Studies using methods as varied as structural equation modeling (Crisp, 2010) and qualitative approaches (Deil-Amen, 2011; Orozco, Alvarez, & Gutkin, 2010) find that strong social relationships encourage integration, a sense of comfort on campus, and connectedness to college. Second, interviews with students consistently underscore the ways that strong social relationships provide important information (Orozco et al., 2010). Deil-Amen (2011) and Karp, Hughes, and O'Gara (2010) found that community college students' social relationships with peers are often "functional," focusing on the provision of academic or navigational help, rather than socialization.

Recent studies of interventions encouraging social relationships demonstrate their importance for improving student success. Studies of learning communities, which create social relationships by grouping students in "linked" classes, find positive outcomes for the time that students are enrolled in the program (Visher, Weiss, Weissman, Rudd, & Wathington, 2012). However, these impacts fade (Visher et al., 2012). This fade-out effect may occur, in part, because student connections to their peers become weaker once they move beyond the learning community structure (Schnee, 2014), implying that (a) social relationships are important and (b) interventions seeking to encourage this mechanism need to be long term.

Karp et al. (2010) found that students who had strong networks of social relationships were more likely to report being integrated into their college environment. Integrated students, in turn, were more likely to make progress toward a degree. In another study, lower level math students were assigned mentors who provided them with information and served as "go-to" individuals for any problems that arose during the semester (Visher, Butcher, & Cerna, 2010); part-time students and developmental math students had improved outcomes as a result.

Finding ways to promote meaningful social relationships for nontraditional students can be challenging. One approach is to integrate relationship-building into students' academic coursework. Deil-Amen (2011) found that "socio-academic integrative moments," which combine academic and social interaction, can be powerful for commuter students. Tovar (2015) found that meeting with faculty outside of class had a small but positive influence on self-reported grade point average (GPA) for Latino/a students.

Clarifying Aspirations and Enhancing Commitment. There is a body of qualitative work indicating that college students, particularly those attending community colleges, are strongly oriented toward the utility of postsecondary education (Cox, 2009). They need to understand why they are expected to learn the content of their courses and how it relates to their future goals (Booth et al., 2013). Survey and correlational studies find that having clear goals and being able to make a connection between students' courses and future career is related to retention (Luke, Redekop, & Burgin, 2015), GPA, and persistence (Nakajima, Dembo, & Mossle, 2012).

The corollary of these findings is that activities that help students understand why they are learning what they are learning can improve their commitment and persistence. Thus, under the right circumstances, advising can improve student outcomes (Bahr, 2008). When advising is sustained, personalized, and focused on helping students clarify their goals and develop realistic programs of study, it is related to improved outcomes, particularly for part-time and developmental education students (Visher et al., 2010).

Unfortunately, advising in community colleges is often underresourced, and many students do not experience high-quality advising that allows them to engage in goal setting and long-term planning (Karp, 2013). Research has found, however, that other approaches to clarifying aspirations and enhancing commitment may also be impactful. For example, Tovar (2015) found that discussing career goals with instructors was related to higher self-reported GPAs for Latino/a students. Moreover, not discussing career issues with advisors was related to lower self-reported GPAs. Using technology to supplement advising may also help students set goals and create commitment: at Austin Community College, students who use an online planning tool to create clear degree plans have higher rates of persistence than similar students who do not use the tool (Civitas Learning, 2015).

Student success courses, which often focus on goal setting and planning, have also been shown to help improve student outcomes, including improved grades, retention, and completion rates (Cho & Karp, 2013; Yamasaki, 2010). Though some random assignment studies have found that the early gains shown by student success course participants fade over time (Rutschow, Cullinan, & Welbeck, 2012), this may be due to the inconsistent and often superficial implementation of the guidance aspect of the success course curriculum (Karp et al., 2012).

A particularly promising study comes from outside of the U.S. community college setting. Schippers and colleagues (Schippers, Scheepers, & Peterson, 2015) found that European students who participated in an intervention designed to help them develop clear and specific goals, plans for achieving those goals, and strategies for addressing obstacles earned more credits and persisted at higher rates than nonparticipants. The impact was stronger for minority and male students.

Developing College Know-How.   There are unwritten rules that successful community college students internalize and master, such as how to engage in academic culture and how to ask for help (Karp & Bork, 2014; Orozco et al., 2010). Qualitative research confirms that entering community college students frequently do not know these rules and struggle in school until they learn them (Campa, 2013). It should be noted that interventions aimed at developing college know-how do not ask students to choose between their home cultures and college culture. Rather, they provide students with strategies to successfully meet the hidden but very real expectations to which college students are held.

Interventions focused on developing students' college know-how are relatively new but an emerging body of research demonstrates that teaching students how to approach the collegiate environment can improve outcomes. In one study (Heller & Marchant, 2015), students in a psychology course were provided with strategies to help them identify key concepts and prioritize their studying. Students exposed to these resources had higher exam scores and course grades than similar students who did not receive such assistance. Another study finds that a first-year seminar that provides students with an orientation to college, practice in using support skills, and assistance in learning how to navigate the college environment improves persistence and grades for up to two years after course completion (Karp, Raufman, Efthimiou, & Ritze, 2016). Additional evidence comes from the positive relationship between student success course participation and improved student outcomes, given that these courses often focus on helping students gain college know-how (Cho & Karp, 2013; Yamasaki, 2010).

Recent research also extends the concept of college know-how to encompass students' self-perceptions. This work underscores the importance of students' understanding how to confront feelings of dislocation, challenge, and difference and reframe them so that they do not interfere with their ability to engage in academic tasks (Yeager & Walton, 2011). Such reframing is particularly important for first-generation and low-income students who are particularly likely to feel that they do not belong in college. In one intervention, in which new students were exposed to others' feelings of discomfort in college and asked to reflect on their own experiences (Walton & Cohen, 2011), African-American students in the treatment group had higher GPAs than African Americans in the control group. The positive effects lasted for 3 years. Though this study was conducted in an elite 4-year institution, it has implications and relevance for the community college sector as well.

Making College Life Feasible.   Community college students face an array of challenges, many of which cannot be anticipated or are short term in nature. They nonetheless serve as barriers to success, as students become concerned with solving these day-to-day issues and cannot focus on school to the extent they would like to or should (Chaplot, Cooper, Johnstone, & Karandjeff, 2015). In analyzing reasons for course withdrawal, Michalski (2014) found that of 11 reasons for withdrawal, the top 4 involved nonacademic reasons such as a conflict with work schedules. Another study (Maroto, Snelling, & Linck, 2015) found that over half of the students at two community colleges were "food insecure," meaning that they have limited or uncertain access to nutritionally adequate and safe food. Food insecurity was associated with lower GPAs.

Services that make college life feasible, then, serve to help students deal with small obstacles that, left unaddressed, might become large enough to stymie progress toward a degree. Interventions that focus on making college life feasible are relatively new, and many are small scale. Therefore, the evidence supporting this mechanism is still emergent; it is, however, growing.

Restructuring financial aid so that it is disbursed throughout the semester ("aid like a paycheck") had promising results in a pilot program and is currently undergoing a larger scale evaluation (Ware, Weissman, & McDermott, 2013). Emergency financial assistance, which provides small, short-term grants for students facing unexpected financial crises, appears to help students remain enrolled in college (Geckler, 2008). This approach, too, has been expanded as a result of its early promise.

Some interventions aimed at making college life feasible help students access services outside of the college, for example helping them apply for Supplemental Nutrition Assistance Program and Temporary Assistance for Needy Families benefits, health insurance, childcare, and transportation subsidies. For example, one college trained advisors to assess students' need for benefits and referred eligible students to a dedicated "benefits access coach." Students were also able to sign up for benefits on campus kiosks. At this college, students receiving benefits enrolled for more terms and earned more credits than similar students who did not receive benefits (Price, Long, Quast, McMaken, & Kioukis, 2014).

Holistic Nonacademic Support

The preceding section identified four mechanisms for supporting students: creating social relationships, clarifying aspirations and enhancing commitment, developing college know-how, and making college life feasible. The importance of these mechanisms continues to be substantiated by research: interventions that encourage these processes are positively related to improved student outcomes. However, in the past 5 years, new programming and evaluation have underscored their interconnected and synergistic nature.

Colleges are increasingly taking a multifaceted and holistic approach to student support. Rather than focus on one or two mechanisms, new approaches encourage three or even all four. This makes intuitive sense: student needs are not monolithic, so why should interventions be? This approach is also research based: constructs such as integration and development of college know-how are interrelated and often serve as mediating, rather than direct, influences on student persistence (Nakajima et al., 2012). It also aligns with broader community college reform efforts, which increasingly focus on redesigning the entire student experience rather than implementing isolated programs (Bailey, Jaggars, & Jenkins, 2015).

Many multifaceted support initiatives are new. However, the early research is strong and promising. This section reviews promising examples illustrating how colleges are redesigning student support to holistically address the four mechanisms described in this chapter.

Perhaps the most dramatic example of a holistic approach to nonacademic support can be found at Guttman Community College, a brand-new college opened in 2012 as part of the City University of New York (CUNY). Guttman is structured to ensure that all its students encounter the four nonacademic support mechanisms. Relationships come from a cohort model in which first-year students are required to enroll full time and take all their courses with the same group of students, coupled with peer mentoring and assigned advisors. Guttman students clarify their aspirations and increase their commitment to school via a required first-year course called "Ethnographies of Work," which helps students explore major and career options. Students participate in mandatory group advising and regular individual meetings with their advisor in order to help them develop college know-how. Regular meetings among faculty and success advocates enable Guttman staff and faculty to identify struggling students and connect them to needed services in a timely manner, thereby helping make college persistence more feasible.

Guttman Community College has only had two graduating classes. Its first cohort had a 2-year graduation rate of 28%, well above the average for CUNY community colleges overall (Guttman Community College, n.d.). The 3-year graduation rate for this cohort was just under 50% (Guttman Community College, n.d.). Although it must be acknowledged that Guttman enrolls a disproportionately high proportion of traditional-aged students and is small in size, it also enrolls a high proportion of students from minority backgrounds, 80% of whom receive need-based aid. Thus, although not generalizable, these outcomes are suggestive of the potential holistic supports have to help students obtain a college credential.

Another example comes from Chicago, where The City Colleges of Chicago have undergone a "reinvention" that restructures curricula while simultaneously integrating multiple nonacademic support mechanisms. Newly streamlined curricular options aid in program planning while simultaneously focusing advising conversations on students' long-term academic and career goals. The redesign also includes mandatory advising aimed at creating strong relationships among students and advisors and an early warning system to identify struggling students so that advisors can connect them to just-in-time services. Though too new for rigorous evaluation, early results indicate that college completion rates in Chicago have doubled (City Colleges of Chicago, n.d.).

But what if a college or system can't recreate itself from scratch? CUNY's Accelerated Studies in Associate Programs (ASAP) provides students with the opportunity to engage in all four support mechanisms but within the context of traditional community college structures. Students attend classes in cohorts, have dedicated advisors with whom they meet biweekly to discuss academic and career goals, and have access to supplemental support, such as metrocards. A rigorous random assignment study found that after 3 years, ASAP students earned more credits, were more likely to graduate, and were more likely to transfer to a 4-year college than similar students who did not participate (Scrivener et al., 2015). ASAP participants had a 3-year graduation rate of 40%, compared to 20% for the control group.

Reformers are also refining traditional student success programs to ensure that they encourage multiple mechanisms. For example, Bronx

New Directions for Community Colleges • DOI: 10.1002/cc

Community College redesigned its student success course to focus on helping students create relationships through mandatory and dedicated advising while developing college know-how through the use of embedded peer mentors and teaching college norms and knowledge. The redesigned course also helped students clarify their goals and create commitment to college by linking student success content to academic subjects, such as psychology and history.

Early results are positive. Participating students had higher grades, earned more credits, and persisted at greater rates than similar nonparticipants (Karp et al., 2016). Moreover, unlike studies of other student success courses, the early advantage was maintained over time, with participants earning better grades and having higher persistence rates up to 2.5 years after enrolling the course.

Similarly, ensuring that learning communities are more than simply linked courses can increase their efficacy. In a study of six learning communities conducted by the National Center for Postsecondary Research, one learning community created social relationships via linked courses but also helped students gain college know-how via enhanced advising and a student success course and made college life more feasible via textbook vouchers. The impact of participation on progression toward a degree was larger at this site than at others in the study (Visher et al., 2012); subsequent follow-up research found that the positive impact on credit accrual was sustained for up to 7 years (Weiss et al., 2014).

Implications and Conclusions

This chapter reviewed and refined Karp's 2011 model of nonacademic support. Evidence from the past 5 years supports the four mechanisms identified in the framework: helping students gain social connections, understand college, clarify their aspirations, and overcome seemingly small obstacles can help them stay enrolled and earn a credential. The recent research implies, however, that we cannot think of "nonacademic support" as a set of stand-alone mechanisms. Instead, we need to acknowledge that just as students' needs vary, necessary forms of support are likely to vary as well. Recent evidence therefore strongly suggests that programs should not encourage one or even two of the mechanisms.

Obviously, not every college is going to start from scratch like Guttman Community College. Scaling reforms like Chicago's or programs like ASAP will be challenging, although the payoff to doing so is likely large. However, the research reviewed here provides insights that colleges can leverage as they reconsider and redesign their own support structures.

Multifaceted Support Matters. The research evidence provides a strong rationale for investing in intensive, intrusive, and holistic supports for community college students. ASAP, for example, is expensive on a per-student-basis but costs less per graduate than traditional associate degree programs (Levin & Garcia, 2013). This evidence can help college personnel make the case to policy makers and funders that investment in student support services will pay off. It can also help college personnel generate buy-in for the hard reform work that often accompanies the scaling-up of holistic support structures.

Nonacademic Support Needs to Be Sustained.   Most of the promising interventions highlighted in the final section of this chapter are long term rather than the typical one-semester intervention. Students' needs change over time, and the mechanisms most meaningful to an individual student are likely to differ at different points in time. Therefore, interventions need to be sustained, catching students when they need help, and strategic, connecting students with the type of support they need when they need it. Short-term interventions do not appear to provide the multifaceted and dynamic support required to maximize the four nonacademic support mechanisms.

Multifaceted Supports Need to Be Intrusive.   Students are often unaware of the nonacademic help they need, particularly with regard to college know-how and clarifying their aspirations. Moreover, they may view the use of support services as an admission that they "do not belong in college" or are somehow deficient. Making nonacademic support an integral part of every student's experience, so that students are forced to encounter them, means that all students will receive help, even if they think they do not need it. Moreover, it moves support services away from a deficit model and toward one that views all students as in need of some assistance.

Holistic Support Does Not Need to Come from a Program.   Bringing faculty and other personnel into the support ecosystem, as many of the holistic interventions described here do, can help students encounter nonacademic support mechanisms more often, more organically, and more cost-effectively. Faculty are particularly important, because they already have relationships with students. College faculty can be "deputized" to be support personnel even as they teach, by being trained in pedagogies that encourage relationship-building and help students develop their cultural capital or college skills. For example, English faculty might be taught how to bring in lessons about cultural capital into their courses. Math faculty might find ways to use the Free Application for Federal Student Aid in their courses to help students learn math skills while also being exposed to the financial aid process. The Heller and Marchant (2015) study described earlier demonstrates that metacognitive skill-building can be integrated into academic courses successfully and with positive impacts on student outcomes.

The attention paid to nonacademic support has grown immensely since 2011. It is clear that this type of support is essential for student success and that colleges are engaging in new, intensive experiments in providing it. The biggest take-away from the research is that there are four nonacademic mechanisms that influence student success, but that these mechanisms work best together. As such, nonacademic support needs to be holistic, multifaceted, and integrated into students' daily lives.

Acknowledgments

This research was funded by the Bill & Melinda Gates Foundation. This chapter is an update of Karp's (2011) CCRC Working Paper, *Towards a New Understanding of Non-Academic Support: Four Mechanisms Encouraging Positive Student Outcomes in the Community College*. CCRC colleagues Nikki Edgecombe, David Blazar, and Madeline Weiss were instrumental in examining the empirical studies considered in that version of the paper.

References

Bahr, P. R. (2008). Cooling out in the community college: What is the effect of academic advising on students' chances of success? *Research in Higher Education, 49*(8), 704–732.

Bailey, T. B., Jaggars, S. S., & Jenkins, D. (2015). *Redesigning America's community colleges: A clearer path to student success.* Cambridge, MA: Harvard University Press.

Booth, K., Cooper, D., Karandjeff, K., Large, M., Pellegrin, N., Purnell, R., … Willett, T. (2013). *Using student voices to redefine support: What community college students say institutions, instructors and others can do to help them success.* Sacramento, CA: The RP Group.

Braxton, J. M., Sullivan, A. V. S., & Johnson, R. M., Jr. (1997). Appraising Tinto's theory of college student departure. In J. C. Smart (Ed.), *Higher education: Handbook of theory and research* (Vol. 12, pp. 107–164). New York, NY: Agathon Press.

Campa, B. (2013). Pedagogies of survival: Cultural resources to foster resilience among Mexican-American community college students. *Community College Journal of Research and Practice, 37*(6), 433–452.

Chaplot, P., Cooper, D., Johnstone, R., & Karandjeff, K. (2015). *Beyond financial aid: How colleges can strengthen the financial stability of low-income students and improve student outcomes.* Indianapolis, IN: Lumina Foundation.

Cho, S. W., & Karp, M. M. (2013). Student success courses in the community college: Early enrollment and educational outcomes. *Community College Review, 41*(1), 86–103.

Civitas Learning. (2015). *Designing and implementing a transformed advising model: Austin Community College.* Austin, TX: Author.

City Colleges of Chicago. (n.d). *City Colleges of Chicago fact sheet.* Retrieved from http://www.ccc.edu/menu/Pages/City-Colleges-of-Chicago-Fact-Sheet-.aspx

Cox, R. D. (2009). *The college fear factor: How students and professors misunderstand one another.* Cambridge, MA: Harvard University Press.

Crisp, G. (2010). The impact of mentoring on the success of community college students. *Review of Higher Education, 34*(1), 39–60.

Deil-Amen, R. (2011). Socio-academic integrative moments: Rethinking academic and social integration among two-year college students in career-related programs. *Journal of Higher Education, 82*(1), 54–91.

Farrington, C. A., Roderick, M., Allensworth, E., Nagaoka, J., Keyes, T. S., Johnson, D. W., & Beechum, N. O. (2012). *Teaching adolescents to become learners: The role of noncognitive factors in shaping school performance, a critical literature review.* Chicago, IL: The University of Chicago Consortium on Chicago School Research.

Geckler, C. (2008). *Helping community college students cope with financial emergencies: Lessons from the Dreamkeepers and Angel Fund Emergency Financial Aid programs.* New York, NY: MDRC.

Guttman Community College. (n.d). *Fast facts.* Retrieved from http://guttman.cuny.edu/about/fast-facts/

Hatch, D. K., & Bohlig, E. M. (2016). An empirical typology of the latent programmatic structure of promising practices at community colleges. *Research in Higher Education,* 57(1), 72–98. doi:10.1007/s11162-015-9379-6

Heller, M. L., & Marchant, G. J. (2015). Facilitating self-regulated learning skills and achievement with a strategic content learning approach. *Community College Journal of Research and Practice,* 39(9), 808–818.

Karp, M. M. (2011). *Toward a new understanding of academic support: Four mechanisms encouraging positive student outcomes in the community college.* (Assessment of Evidence Series). CCRC Working Paper No. 28. New York, NY: Columbia University, Teachers College, Community College Research Center.

Karp, M. M. (2013). *Entering a program: Helping students make academic and career decisions.* CCRC Working Paper No. 59. New York, NY: Columbia University, Teachers College, Community College Research Center.

Karp, M. M., Bickerstaff, S., Rucks-Ahidiana, Z., Bork, R. H., Barragan, M., & Edgecombe, N. (2012). *College 101 courses for applied learning and student success.* CCRC Working Paper #49. New York, NY: Columbia University, Teachers College, Community College Research Center.

Karp, M. M., & Bork, R. H. (2014). "They never told me what to expect, so I didn't know what to do": Defining and clarifying the role of a community college student. *Teachers College Record,* 116(5), 1–40.

Karp, M. M., Hughes, K. L., & O'Gara, L. (2010). An exploration of Tinto's integration framework for community college students. *Journal of College Student Retention,* 12(1), 69–86.

Karp, M. M., Raufman, J., Efthimiou, C., & Ritze, N. (2016). Redesigning a student success course for sustained impact: Early outcomes findings. *Community College Journal of Research and Practice.* doi:10.1080/10668926.2016.1152929

Levin, H. M., & Garcia, E. (2013). *Benefit-cost analysis of Accelerated Study in Associate Programs (ASAP) of the City University of New York.* New York, NY: Columbia University, Teachers College, Center for Benefit-Cost Studies in Education.

Luke, C., Redekop, F., & Burgin, C. (2015). Psychological factors in community college student retention. *Community College Journal of Research and Practice,* 39(3), 222–234.

Maroto, M. E., Snelling, A., & Linck, H. (2015). Food insecurity among community college students: Prevalence and association with grade point average. *Community College Journal of Research and Practice,* 39(6), 515–526.

Michalski, G. V. (2014). In their own words: A text analytics investigation of college course attrition. *Community College Journal of Research and Practice,* 38(9), 811–826.

Nakajima, M. A., Dembo, M. H., & Mossler, R. (2012). Student persistence in community college. *Community College Journal of Research and Practice,* 36(8), 591–613.

Orozco, G. L., Alvarez, A. N., & Gutkin, T. (2010). Effective advising of diverse students in community colleges. *Community College Journal of Research and Practice,* 34(9), 717–737.

Pascarella, E. T., & Terenzini, P. T. (2005). *How college affects students: A third decade of research* (Vol. 2). San Francisco, CA: Jossey-Bass.

Price, D., Long, M., Quast, S. S., McMaken, J., & Kioukis, G. (2014). *Public benefits and community colleges: Lessons from the Benefits Access for College Completion Evaluation.* Philadelphia, PA: DVP-Praxis and OMG Center for Collaborative Learning.

Rutschow, E. Z., Cullinan, D., & Welbeck, R. (?012). *Keeping students on course: An impact study of a student success course at Guilford Technical Community College.* New York, NY: MDRC.

Schippers, M. C., Scheepers, A. W. A., & Peterson, J. B. (2015). A scalable goal-setting intervention closes both the gender and ethnic minority achievement gap. *Palgrave Communications, 1.* doi:10.1057/palcomms.2015.14

Schnee, E. (2014). "A foundation for something bigger": Community college students' experience of remediation in the context of a learning community. *Community College Review, 42*(3), 242–261.

Scrivener, S., Weiss, M. J., Ratledge, A., Rudd, T., Sommo, C., & Fresques, H. (2015). *Doubling graduation rates: Three-year effects of CUNY's Accelerated Studies in Associate Programs (ASAP) for developmental education students.* New York, NY: MDRC.

Tinto, V. (1993). *Leaving college: Rethinking the causes and cures of student attrition* (2nd ed.). Chicago, IL: University of Chicago Press.

Tovar, E. (2015). The role of faculty, counselors, and support programs on Latino/a community college students' success and intent to persist. *Community College Review, 43*(1), 46–71.

Visher, M. G., Butcher, K. F., & Cerna, O. S. (2010). *Guiding developmental math students to campus services: An impact evaluation of the Beacon program at South Texas College.* New York, NY: MDRC.

Visher, M. G., Weiss, M. J., Weissman, E., Rudd, T., & Wathington, H. D. (2012). *The effects of learning communities for students in developmental education: A synthesis of findings from six colleges.* New York, NY: National Center for Postsecondary Research.

Walton, G. M., & Cohen, G. L. (2011). A brief social-belonging intervention improves academic and health outcomes of minority students. *Science, 331*(6023), 1447–1451.

Ware, M., Weissman, E., & McDermott, D. (2013). *Aid like a paycheck: Incremental aid to promote student success.* New York, NY: MDRC.

Weiss, M., Mayer, A., Cullinane, D., Ratledge, A., Sommo, C., & Diamond, J. (2014). *A random assignment of learning communities at Kingsborough Community College: Seven years later.* New York, NY: MDRC.

Yamasaki, K. (2010). *Enrollment in success courses: Credential completion rates and developmental education in the North Carolina Community College System* (Master's thesis). Durham, NC: Sanford School of Public Policy, Duke University.

Yeager, D. S., & Walton, G. M. (2011). Social-psychological interventions in education: They're not magic. *Review of Educational Research, 81*(2), 267–301.

MELINDA MECHUR KARP *is the assistant director of the Community College Research Center (CCRC), Teachers College, Columbia University.*

NEW DIRECTIONS FOR COMMUNITY COLLEGES • DOI: 10.1002/cc

4

This chapter discusses the work of the Center for Community College Student Engagement, highlighting institutes the Center hosts and work that comes from these meetings. Examples of interventions that evolved from the High-Impact Practices Institutes conducted by the Center are provided. The chapter concludes with a discussion about implementation and evaluation practices important to the interpretation of intervention success.

Student Success: Identifying High-Impact Practices

Evelyn N. Waiwaiole, E. Michael Bohlig, Kristine J. Massey

The Center for Community College Student Engagement (the Center), a research and service organization, was established in 2008 through The University of Texas at Austin's College of Education as an umbrella organization for survey research, focus group work, and related services to community and technical colleges interested in improving educational quality through strengthened student engagement and student success. The mission of the Center is to provide important information about effective educational practices in community colleges. The Center assists institutions and policy makers with using information to promote improvements in student learning, persistence, and attainment.

The Center conducts two student surveys annually: the Survey of Entering Student Engagement (*SENSE*) and the Community College Survey of Student Engagement (*CCSSE*). The *CCSSE* instrument, which emerged from the work of the National Survey of Student Engagement, was developed between 2001 and 2004. *SENSE*, developed in 2007, was designed specifically to focus on the "front door" experiences of entering students and help colleges identify areas to improve student engagement and thereby improve student success and persistence.

In response to demand from the community and technical college field, the Community College Faculty Survey of Student Engagement (*CCFSSE*) was developed in 2005. This survey was designed to elicit information on the faculty's perception of students' educational experiences as well as their teaching practices and how they spend their professional time.

NEW DIRECTIONS FOR COMMUNITY COLLEGES, no. 175, Fall 2016 © 2016 Wiley Periodicals, Inc.
Published online in Wiley Online Library (wileyonlinelibrary.com) • DOI: 10.1002/cc.20211

Table 4.1   Thirteen Promising Practices Surveyed in the CCIS

First-year experience
Learning communities
College orientation
Student success course
Accelerated courses or fast-track programs in developmental/remedial education
Academic goal setting and planning
Experiential learning beyond the classroom
Tutoring
Supplemental instruction
Assessment and placement
Registration before classes begin
Class attendance
Alert and intervention

Most recently, in 2011, the Center undertook a 3-year project to identify and promote high-impact practices. The Center identified 13 practices (see Table 4.1) that, based on the literature, held promise for improving student success. To assess the prevalence, institutional implementation, and policies associated with these practices, the Center developed the Community College Institutional Survey (CCIS).

For a more complete description of the Center's surveys and work, visit www.cccse.org.

Research to Practice

As part of its mission and to help colleges use data, the Center invites member colleges to participate in events that are intensely focused on data, including Center survey results. Each of these institutes and workshops employs a working model to help colleges identify priorities and strategies for increasing student success and to initiate important discussions crucial to carrying out this work.

The Center hosted three High-Impact Practices (HIP) institutes between April 2013 and March 2015, which were attended by 25 colleges from across the country including St. Louis Community College (STLCC) and Coastal Bend College (CBC). Their experiences at the March 2013 institute, the short-term action plans developed at the institutes, and results based on those plans are highlighted. Before delving into these stories, it will be helpful to understand the context of the HIP institutes.

Participating colleges engaged in a 2½ day in-depth review of data from multiple sources and discussions of the college's policies and practices. Colleges were encouraged to include the president, chief academic officer, chief student services offices, lead institutional researcher, and a faculty leader on their institute teams.

Colleges were provided with homework assignments to complete prior to the institute that created a tailored institutional agenda or conversation

NEW DIRECTIONS FOR COMMUNITY COLLEGES • DOI: 10.1002/cc

for the institute. Institute homework included a review of CCIS data, Center survey data (*CCSSE* and/or *SENSE*) and institutional cohort data over a 6-year period. College teams reviewed the CCIS data about institutional policy and then compared it to *CCSSE* or *SENSE* data about student participation in the practices. Another part of the homework compared *CCSSE* data to *CCFSSE* data, if they were available, to look at faculty perspectives in relation to student perspectives and institutional policy. Each college team came prepared, having previously assessed the work the college had done to improve student success, and ready to build upon the existing student success agenda. At the conclusion of the institute, college teams developed a short-term action plan to support the continuing work toward a data-informed and evidence-based student success agenda. These action plans identified (a) three priorities, (b) the desired outcomes for the priorities, (c) activities and tasks that accompanied each priority, (d) the person responsible for each priority, (e) a timeline, (f) necessary resources, and (g) potential issues or concerns. Following the institute, colleges submitted the completed short-term action plans to the Center.

The authors recently followed up with St. Louis Community College and Coastal Bend College, two colleges that attended the 2013 High-Impact Practices Institute to learn about post-institute progress. Both colleges focused on the entering student experience; their postinstitute progress is described next.

St. Louis Community College (STLCC).   One of the most challenging aspects of changing the student experience through HIPs is to take a truly comprehensive, systemic approach to influencing overall student success. When STLCC initiated its work on redesigning the student learning experience in 2010–2011, a careful examination of data revealed that fewer than one of every two students (45% in fall 2011) were returning from fall to fall. The fall-to-spring retention rate at that time was 70%. Collectively, the college determined that it could not affect any other student success metric if it could not first affect retention for *all* first-time-in-college (FTIC) students.

Over several years, ongoing studies revealed that the student experience varied widely across the four campuses that compose the STLCC district. With that reality in mind, the college set about the task of redesigning the first-semester experience. The process of further clarifying objectives of a redesigned experience was advanced through participation in the 2013 High-Impact Practices Institute. Drawing upon input from students, faculty, and staff, participants from both academic and student affairs engaged in exercises that identified student learning outcomes from the time students first "touch" the community college to their completion of the first semester. The result of that collaborative effort was the identification of four components of a redesigned first-semester experience: New Student Registration Workshop (NSRW), New Student Orientation (Orientation LIVE: Arrive and Thrive), a student success course (Smart Start), and a retention-focused faculty initiative titled First 4 Weeks (F4W). Redesign teams for each strategy were identified, and the careful work of development and implementation was begun.

Components of Redesign.   The college took seriously its directive not to "tweak around the edges" but rather to make radical changes that would affect the greatest number of students possible with its adopted HIPs. All strategies were fully implemented in fall 2012. As of spring 2015, over 17,000 FTIC students have experienced the redesigned first-semester experience at STLCC.

New Student Registration Workshop.   This component is a 90-minute mandatory experience for all FTIC students who have completed the required steps prior to registration. (Typical of the student population, FTIC students at STLCC in fall 2014 were 52% female, 51% White, and 37% Black, with smaller percentages of Asian, Hispanic, and multiracial students (4%, 3%, and 4%, respectively.) Students who are new to college are required to attend this session in order to register for classes. It consists of

- presentation on terminology, payment options, college resources, and services;
- academic advising to plan the student's first semester; and
- registration to introduce students to technology and teach them how to register for classes.

Orientation LIVE: Arrive and Thrive.   This component is a 2-hour program for FTIC students. This interactive experience is facilitated by student leaders and offers a consistent student success message at every STLCC campus location. Students are introduced to the demands and responsibilities of being a college student. They become aware of college resources and services and learn how and where to access those services. Additionally, they are introduced to technology tools required of STLCC students. Students are required to sign up for an orientation session during the mandatory NSRW; however, because of several constraints, students who do not attend an orientation session are still allowed to attend classes. Although early phases of implementation did not track data for all orientation sessions, records indicate that just under 9,000 of the 17,000 FTIC students have attended new student orientations since fall 2012.

Smart Start.   This component is STLCC's student success program. Smart Start Student Success is a mandatory three-credit-hour offering for students who place into developmental English and/or reading. Among its many outcomes, the course focuses on self-awareness for students, skills and attitudes necessary for success in college, time management and goal setting, identification of a program of study, and education as a lifelong priority. The course is extremely important as a strategy for reaching minority students, as they are disproportionately represented in this course (60% Black, 31% White).

First 4 Weeks.   This component is a list of possible classroom activities/approaches to promote student engagement during the first weeks of the semester. The following are a few examples of these strategies that faculty are encouraged to use:

- Create an assignment to demonstrate that students are able to log into Blackboard, as well as update their contact information in Banner
- Have students email the faculty member using their college email account
- Share their passion for the subject
- Explain the context or "big picture" of the course and how it is relevant in students' academic, professional, and personal lives
- Let students know what they need to do to be successful in their course
- For online classes, hold a class meeting via Collaborate in Blackboard

Faculty are asked to choose from a list of identified activities and approaches and to commit to implementing at least four of them during the first four weeks of the semester.

The Results.   After several years of declining trends in retention prior to the redesign of the first-semester experience, the college saw its first increase in fall-to-fall retention for the fall 2012 cohort of students—from 45% to 48%; however, no increase from fall to spring was observed. For the fall 2013 cohort of students, fall-to-spring retention increased from 70% to 73% and fall-to-fall retention increased from 48% to 50%. The fall-to-spring retention rate for the fall 2014 cohort remained consistent at 73%. These initial results in retention suggest that the efforts to address the student success agenda may be having a positive impact.

Next Steps.   After nearly three full years of implementation of the redesigned first-semester experience, the college is continuing its effort of optimizing the student learning experience by creating a student success team focused more broadly on the first-year experience. All four components of the first-semester experience will be addressed for continuous improvement/redesign as this work moves into a more mature phase of analysis of available data and demonstrated student learning outcomes.

Both quantitative and qualitative analysis of the Smart Start course occurs each semester, and a continuous improvement team analyzes and acts upon results of the assessments that are conducted by making course changes and improvements in required professional development for all instructors who teach the course.

For a more complete description of this program and the evaluation methods, contact the college's Institutional Research and Planning office.

Coastal Bend College (CBC).   The April 2013 High-Impact Practices Institute was the impetus for improving the orientation program at CBC. Administrators and faculty attended the institute in search of answers and resources to improve the orientation program.

NEW DIRECTIONS FOR COMMUNITY COLLEGES • DOI: 10.1002/cc

The existing orientation program was not effective in part because it was reaching less than a quarter of all new students. In fall 2013, only 330 of the 1,373 FTIC students (24%) attended orientation. When students were asked to provide feedback on the program, many indicated that they did not realize that they were attending orientation. In fact, many students and family members believed the CBC orientation program was a gathering to eat free food and get a free CBC T-shirt. This alerted the college that students were not receiving the college knowledge necessary to be successful on the first day of instruction. A review team concluded that the orientation program had to change.

In February 2012, President Espinoza convened a team of administrators, faculty, and staff to drastically change and improve the orientation program at CBC. She introduced the team to the college as the Quality Enhancement Leadership Team. Their responsibility was to meet monthly, review data regarding orientation, and make recommendations to improve orientation. This team produced a pilot orientation program for new CBC students labeled Cougar Days. The team identified the time and days to deliver this program at each of the four CBC sites in July 2014.

In fall 2014, the team met several times to discuss improvements and modifications of the pilot orientation program. One change was to make orientation mandatory. This change had a large impact the following fall: orientation participation increased from 656 in 2013–2014 (38.4% of 1,709 FTIC students) to 1,039 in 2014–2015 (75.2% of 1,382 FTIC students).

To better inform students about orientation, the Media and Marketing Office developed strategies for intentional marketing. The Cougar Days were published on the main CBC webpage, posters were distributed at each of the sites, and advisors informed students during registration sessions. Students were also sent email and text messages prior to the event.

Orientation was offered to students in three formats:

- Cougar Days Orientation was offered a few weeks prior to the first week of class. This campuswide collaborative effort was a full day of programming and events. Faculty, staff, and administrators came together to organize and implement the sessions in which students received hands-on training on the student learning management system, email, student portal, student services, online resources, and business services.
- Online Orientation was also offered to students who were not on campus and were only enrolled in online classes. Students also received training on the student learning management system, email, student portal, student services, online resources, and business services.
- Face-to-Face 1-hour orientation workshops were also offered throughout the semester for students who were not able to attend Cougar Days or were not comfortable with the online modality. These workshops were conducted by advisors.

NEW DIRECTIONS FOR COMMUNITY COLLEGES • DOI: 10.1002/cc

The most attended orientation modality was Cougar Days in FY 2013–14. A total of 656 students attended all modalities combined. Cougar Days alone had 578 or 88% of the total attendees. The orientations offered on-line and throughout the semester were the least attended ($N = 78$). Students who did not participate in any Cougar Days or the online orientation were asked to participate in the 1-hour orientation workshops scheduled throughout the semester.

Part of the evaluation process for the orientation program included a post-assessment. Review of these data found that the questions on the post-assessment were not aligned with the content of the Cougar Days program. The Quality Enhancement Leadership Team revised the post-assessment instrument to better align it with the program content, and the revised assessment will be used in the 2015–16 Cougar Days program.

Even though the post-assessment instrument was not fully aligned with the orientation content, analysis of the pre- to post-assessment of student knowledge revealed a substantial increase: Students who attended the face-to-face orientation settings showed a 75% increase in knowledge from pre- to post-assessment, and those participating in the online orientation showed a 68% increase.

Evaluation of CBC's orientation FY 2013–14 efforts found that students who attended orientation have higher grade point averages (GPAs) and persistence rates than students who did not attend orientation. First, orientation attendees had an overall GPA of 2.8 compared with non-attendees who had an overall GPA of 2.4. Second, the persistence rate of students who attended orientation was 78% vs. non-attending students at 62%.

Taking time at the 2013 High-Impact Practices Institute to review data, reflect, and evaluate the colleges' orientation efforts fostered an environment for discussion that led to a plan for improvement. Student success is improving, but more work is yet to come.

For a more complete description of this program and the evaluation methods, contact the college's Institutional Effectiveness and Accreditation office.

Taking an Institute Back to the College

Many college teams have attended the Center's institutes and made great progress with their student success agendas. The time at the institute allows teams to spend concentrated, uninterrupted energy looking at data and having facilitated conversations on how to help more students—all students—succeed. What is critical, however, is that the conversation not stop when the institute concludes. At the Center, we encourage team members to think of the institute as a model that can be taken to the campus and hosted with greater stakeholder involvement. We encourage teams to use the *CCIS Campus Discussion Guide: Exploring High-Impact Practices* (http://www.ccsse.org/docs/CCIS_DiscussionGuide.pdf) and unpack policies and practices that are in place alongside institutional and Center data and engage others in a rich conversation about what is working and what is not.

After reviewing existing practices, ideas for new practices will surface; however, finding practices that are beneficial for most students is not a process that can be rushed. As with anything new, it takes time to fine tune programs and for all involved in the implementation to become familiar and comfortable with the components. There is a fine balance between the need for quick results and a long-lasting solution. Fullan, Cuttress, & Kilcher (2005) noted that with anything new, especially complex processes, challenges will emerge early on that will likely be reflected in an "implementation dip" as those involved in the intervention become familiar with the components and processes (Fullan, 2002; Fullan et al., 2005). It is, therefore, important not to react to early results if they do not show expected outcomes by eliminating the intervention and searching for something new; the process should start with a strong implementation design that can capture the data necessary to facilitate an understanding of why the results emerged and, where necessary, to identify program aspects that need adjustment.

Given the investment—both financial and human—in bringing an intervention into practice begs the investment in the design, implementation, and evaluation of an intervention that can generate crucial data for an informed decision about whether it is a good fit and should be brought to scale or that it is not the right program for the institution. Just as St. Louis Community College and Coastal Bend College demonstrated modifications and improvements over time, practices are dynamic and depend on continuous data review to inform modifications where necessary, ideally leading to enhanced student success.

Implementation to Evaluation: Next Steps

As conversations about practices continue at colleges, regardless of whether they started at a Center-sponsored institute or elsewhere, it is important to remember that implementation and evaluation are essential components of any effort to improve student success. Inclusion of the college's institutional research team, or others at the institution who have the necessary skills, is important; a recurring theme in presentations on higher education interventions at national, state, and regional Association for Institutional Research (AIR) meetings over recent years has been how much stronger program design and evaluation could have been and how many mistakes could have been avoided if institutional researchers had been involved from the outset.

Program design and evaluation are critical and entail a range of tasks and topics, several of which are often completely overlooked or given short shrift and are addressed below. These aspects of program design are highlighted as they are necessary though not sufficient for one to be able to assert that the observed outcome can be attributed to the intervention.

Starting with the end in mind, clearly defining the anticipated outcome is important from several perspectives, not the least of which is that it allows program designers to identify and define program components that target the knowledge and skills necessary for participants to achieve the outcome. Clearly defining these components feeds the development of the programmatic and curricular elements of the intervention, the design of professional development for those responsible for implementing the intervention, and tools for monitoring the implementation. Monitoring the intervention includes not only the assessment of students' skills and knowledge of program content but especially tracking the implementation of key program components.

One frequent and fundamental flaw in evaluation of interventions is that the actual intervention is treated like a black box (Carleton-Hug & Hug, 2010; Conn, 2012; Finney & Moos, 1984); there is little or no monitoring to verify that the intervention is being implemented as designed. Failure to closely monitor the implementation threatens the validity of the outcomes. Without this critical information, it is not possible to verify that the intervention was fully implemented as designed, or which parts were implemented, rendering attribution of outcomes, good or bad, to the intervention inappropriate.

Monitoring the intervention can be an expensive and extremely challenging task. However, securing early buy-in by those involved in the intervention and thinking about monitoring a little differently can help minimize some of the challenges. Implementation monitoring often brings to mind the intrusive picture of an observer sitting in the classroom capturing everything that happens. Although periodic in-person observation by an evaluator is important, especially early on, closely monitoring the intervention throughout the course of the intervention does not have to look like this. If the intervention design includes a set of clearly defined essential components and the frequency with which they should be addressed, these can be translated into a checklist that the instructor can complete in 30 seconds following each class session. The checklist data can then be analyzed to verify that the critical components were delivered per the intervention protocol. These data can also provide important information to the program designers indicating where certain components may not have worked as expected and need to be reevaluated. As Fullan (2002) notes, when implementing a new program, something is bound to not go according to design; closely monitoring the intervention can identify these challenges, provide important information that will allow intervention designers to address challenges early, and adapt the intervention quickly to avoid an extended period of negative outcomes. Is having the individuals responsible for delivering the intervention the "best" way to monitor and validate the program implementation? In short, no; however, those charged with implementing the intervention are professionals committed to student success and, as such, are fully capable of capturing the program components covered during the course of the intervention. After all, monitoring the intervention is all about designing a successful program with the potential for long-lasting results across the entire student population.

The process by which students are selected into the participant and nonparticipant groups has considerable ramifications for being able to assert a causal relationship between participation in the intervention and the outcomes. "As long as there is some non-random process by which students enroll or are chosen for such a program, it may be that any differences between participants and non-participants result from the selection process, not from the program itself" (Bailey & Alfonso, 2005, p. 12). In other words, random assignment provides the strongest design for the most conclusive results. This does require more advanced planning and upfront effort, but the analysis of the program data after the intervention can be less daunting, requiring less sophisticated statistical techniques, and the results will be more generalizable than results based on interventions that use a nonrandom assignment process. One argument frequently asserted against random assignment is that it is not fair to deny some students access to a new intervention while offering it to others. However, because institution-wide or full-scale implementation of new interventions is extremely rare, if not totally absent from the higher educational landscape, some students will experience the program and others will not. Under this reality, random assignment would seem to be no less fair a means of determining who receives the intervention with the added bonus of being the best approach to facilitate the most reliable and most generalizable results.

Conclusion

The time to help students succeed is now and ideas are plentiful. As colleges determine next steps, one approach is to first complete a self-study and have a thorough understanding of what practices are currently in place at the college. The CCIS can provide a starting point for a self-study, although these data must be supplemented with other data sources from your institution. If a college would like to use the CCIS, they can contact the Center (info@cccse.org) for more information.

References

Bailey, T. R., & Alfonso, M. (2005). *Paths to persistence: An analysis of research on program effectiveness at community colleges* (New Agenda Series, Vol. 6, No. 1). Indianapolis, IN: Lumina Foundation.

Carleton-Hug, A., & Hug, J. W. (2010). Challenges and opportunities for evaluating environmental education programs. *Evaluation and Program Planning, 33*(2), 159–164. doi:10.1016/j.evalprogplan.2009.07.005

Conn, V. S. (2012). Unpacking the black box: Countering the problem of inadequate intervention descriptions in research reports. *Western Journal of Nursing Research, 34*(4), 427–433. doi:10.1177/0193945911434627

Finney, J. W., & Moos, R. H. (1984). Environmental assessment and evaluation research: Examples from mental health and substance abuse programs. *Evaluation and Program Planning, 7*(2), 151–167. doi:10.1016/0149-7189(84)90041-7

Fullan, M. (2002). The change leader. *Educational Leadership, 59*(8), 16–20.

Fullan, M., Cuttress, C., & Kilcher, A. (2005). 8 forces for leaders of change. *Journal of Staff Development, 26*(4), 54–64.

EVELYN N. WAIWAIOLE is director of the Center for Community College Student Engagement.

E. MICHAEL BOHLIG is assistant director of research of the Center for Community College Student Engagement.

KRISTINE J. MASSEY is a graduate research assistant at the Center for Community College Student Engagement.

5

This chapter draws from national data to explore unique attributes of first-year seminars in community college contexts as well as high-impact practices that are often connected to them. Findings point to areas of opportunity for practice and directions for future research to better understand how community colleges can be poised to meet the increasing number of demands to support student success in effective ways.

Using Hybridization and Specialization to Enhance the First-Year Experience in Community Colleges: A National Picture of High-Impact Practices in First-Year Seminars

Dallin George Young, Jennifer R. Keup

Community colleges have recently been tasked to assume important functions in higher education, such as enlarging their role as a driver for access to postsecondary education, bearing an increasing share of the responsibility for expanding credentialing rates to meet the Obama administration's college completion agenda, and, in a growing number of states, serving as the primary mechanism to bring underprepared students up to proficiency for college-level work. These forces have caused a shift among community colleges from a focus on simply providing access and service to the community to one of increased student success. However, community college campuses have long been challenged in their efforts to meet these goals by an overrepresentation of students who are historically underrepresented in higher education, in need of developmental and remedial coursework, and possessing other personal, demographic, and academic factors that indicate they are at risk in the higher education context (Center for Community College Student Engagement [CCCSE], 2012, 2015; McClenney, 2011). Thus, it is perhaps not surprising that national figures indicate that almost half of all first-time full-time students in community colleges do not persist to the second year and associate's degree 3-year completion rates range

New Directions for Community Colleges, no. 175, Fall 2016 © 2016 Wiley Periodicals, Inc.
Published online in Wiley Online Library (wileyonlinelibrary.com) • DOI: 10.1002/cc.20212

between 23% and 44% (ACT, 2014; Habley, 2011). The combination of poor retention statistics and a renewed emphasis on student transition, learning, development, and academic performance in the first year and throughout the undergraduate experience has rekindled an interest in the first-year experience (FYE) in community colleges. In particular, one key intervention for colleges in the first year has been the first-year seminar (FYS), a course intentionally designed to facilitate the social and academic transition of first-year students into postsecondary education (Barefoot, 1992).

This chapter presents the FYS in community colleges as one part of a multifaceted approach to providing a high-impact first-year experience. It begins with the background and definition of the FYS and then turns to a discussion of the FYS as key part of a high-impact educational experience in community colleges. Thereafter, national survey data on FYSs provide information as to how community colleges are structuring this intervention to meet the needs of their students. The chapter concludes with a discussion of areas of opportunity for practice to better leverage the FYS in community colleges to support student success.

Definition and Background of the First-Year Seminar

Evidence of student success courses can be found as early as 1877 at Johns Hopkins University and the first student success seminar offered to first-year students for academic credit has been traced to Lees College in 1882 (Barefoot & Fidler, 1996; Gordon, 1989). Across centuries, first-year seminars have been defined as small, highly engaging courses that aim to "enhance the academic and/or social integration of first-year students by introducing them (a) to a variety of specific topics, which vary by seminar type, (b) to essential skills for college success, and (c) to selected processes the most common of which is the creation of a peer support group" (Barefoot, 1992, p. 49). Through the process of introducing new students to these key elements of successful college transitions, FYSs have been found to facilitate a host of student outcomes, including academic achievement and grades; civic engagement; intercultural competence and multicultural awareness; positive relationships with faculty, staff, and peers; involvement on campus; development of academic, interpersonal, and life skills; and persistence and graduation rates (e.g., Brownell & Swaner, 2010; Greenfield, Keup, & Gardner, 2013; Griffin & Romm, 2008; Tobolowsky, Cox, & Wagner, 2005). In the second volume of their encyclopedic review of higher education research, Pascarella & Terenzini (2005) state that FYSs yield "statistically significant and substantial, positive effects on a student's successful transition to college and the likelihood of persistence to the second year as well as on academic performance while in college and on a considerable array of other college experiences" (p. 403). Recent research has indicated that engaging pedagogy and "learning for application" are critical components to the effectiveness, outcomes, and long-term impact of FYSs (Karp et al., 2012;

New Directions for Community Colleges • DOI: 10.1002/cc

Padgett, Keup, & Pascarella, 2013; Porter & Swing, 2006; Swing, 2002). However, these critical features of FYSs have, at times throughout history, been undermined by a sole focus on community building and life skills. Given this drift from a balance of academic, personal, and interpersonal learning objectives for the course, institutional support waned over time until FYSs all but died out in the mid-20th century.

FYSs and other student success interventions, such as service learning and learning communities, experienced a renaissance during the latter phase (i.e., 1960s and 1970s) of the mass era of U.S. higher education (Cohen & Kisker, 2010). Community colleges were a major contributor to this period of higher education history, which was characterized by a focus on access and a massive influx of students from a wide array of personal and academic backgrounds (Boggs, 2011; Cohen & Brawer, 1996). However, although the doors of higher education were thrown open to the diverse masses, a disproportionate number of students were stumbling after walking through the entryway of the hallowed halls of higher education. Thus, higher education institutions rediscovered numerous interventions that had historically been focused on facilitating student learning and success, including FYSs, in order to fulfill their implicit promise to admitted students for the potential of degree completion (Greenfield et al., 2013).

Over the past few decades, FYSs have become almost ubiquitous in higher education. More specifically, national data indicating that between 85% and 95% of all institutions offer at least one section of this course to new students. The proportion of community colleges offering FYS has increased from 71% in 2003 to 86% in 2012 (Tobolowsky, 2005; Young & Hopp, 2014). A recent examination of student success initiatives at community colleges showed that FYSs are one of the three most common institutional support efforts that community colleges engage along with preterm orientation activities for advising and registration and early warning/academic alert systems (Koch, Griffin, & Barefoot, 2014). When their widespread use is coupled with the overwhelming empirical evidence of their positive impact, FYSs represent one of the most promising practices for supporting new student transitions to college.

One potential reason for the extensive adoption of FYSs is that the intervention is particularly tractable and "is flexible enough to meet the growing needs of the changing student demographic" (Gahagan, 2002, p 6). The wide variety of seminar types, objectives, content areas, managerial reporting lines, administrative characteristics, pedagogical approaches, instructional staff, faculty development and support models, and targeted student populations all afford myriad opportunities to tailor the course to each institutional context and even adjust it to specific student subpopulations within that campus setting (Padgett & Keup, 2011; Young & Hopp, 2014). Further, trend analyses of FYS characteristics indicate that the course has introduced greater combinations and customization of seminar types, more delivery methods and instructional models, and greater variety in outcomes and topics to meet the shifting characteristics and needs of students (Tobolowsky & Associates, 2008).

Emergence of First-Year Seminars as a High-Impact Practice

The growth in the base of scholarship and best practice has positioned FYSs well and given them traction in the higher education landscape. Researchers from the Center for Community College Student Engagement provided evidence that FYSs have prominence as an effective educational practice in community colleges, both as part of larger first-year experience programs and in the form of college success courses, which were 2 of the 13 practices identified as educationally effective for student success in community colleges (CCSSE, 2012). Further evidence of institutionalization of FYSs as a critical intervention occurred when they were first on the Association of American Colleges & Universities' (AAC&U's) list of 10 campus practices that lead to strong educational outcomes as part of their Liberal Education and America's Promise (LEAP) project (Kuh, 2008).

FYSs are particularly important among these lists for two reasons. First, they are the only practice that must be, by definition, offered in the first year. As such, they are frequently among the first high-impact practices (HIPs) in which a new student will engage and, thus, often introduce students to college-level work and model standards of quality for other higher education interventions. Second, research and practice provide evidence that the FYS has been a hub or a key delivery point for other HIPs to first-year students in both community college and 4-year contexts, albeit in different ways based on the unique needs and context of the sector and institution. High-impact pedagogical approaches, such as writing-intensive educational experiences, collaborative assignments and projects, and diversity and global learning, are common fixtures in the FYS and they also frequently include service learning, are embedded in a learning community, or are connected to a first-year/summer reading program as a common intellectual experience (Young & Hopp, 2014). However, HIPs were intentionally connected to or included in FYSs at significantly lower rates at community colleges; 4-year institutions had an average of three HIPs offered in conjunction with a FYS compared to two HIPs at community colleges (Young & Hopp, 2014).

Of greatest significance to student populations common in community colleges has been the emphasis on high-impact practices, including FYSs, as a critical vehicle for equity in higher education. Recent studies have shown consistent evidence that, although HIPs are effective educational experiences for all students, "historically underserved students tend to benefit *more* from engaging in educational purposeful activities than majority students" (Kuh, 2008, p. 17). Finally, exposure to multiple high-impact practices, as is often the case with HIPs bundled in the FYS, generated even greater positive impacts among underserved students. In sum, one of "the most valuable finding[s] is the 'equity effects' that appear in students' report of their learning as their success is boosted by HIPs" (Schneider & Albertine, 2013, p. v). As community colleges are frequently gateways into postsecondary education for students who fit into these categories (CCSSE, 2012, 2015; McClenney, 2011), understanding how to better structure the educational environment through interventions, such as FYSs and other associated HIPs, can point to mechanisms to support student success in community colleges and advance an equity agenda in higher education at large.

A National Picture of Features of FYSs in Community Colleges: The National Survey of First-Year Seminars

To illustrate current practice in the United States and to highlight areas of opportunity for creating high-impact environments that support student success in community colleges, we draw on data from the 2012–2013 National Survey of First-Year Seminars (NSFYS) conducted by the National Resource Center for The First-Year Experience and Students in Transition. This national survey included 896 responses from institutions and provided information from about 803 (89.7%) institutions with at least one FYS on campus. A total of 239 responses came from 2-year colleges, of which 206 (86.2%) indicated offering a FYS. This group of 206 2-year institutions forms the sample of community colleges on which the analyses that follow are based. The NSFYS asked respondents to provide information about types of seminars, as well as administration, assessment, instruction, and objectives of these courses. In addition, the survey included a specific focus on which, if any, high-impact practices (as defined by AAC&U and CCSSE) were intentionally included in or connected to the FYS.

An overview of current features of FYS in community colleges provides a sense of how these institutions are serving their students. To that end, this section highlights results from the NSFYS that show how these environments are being constructed. Moreover, because the literature on the characteristics and implementation of HIPs, including the FYS, is predominantly written from the point of view of 4-year institutions, we have included a contrast between 2-year and 4-year structures in our presentation of the information. This is not to cast the FYS in 2-year institutions as something that can be understood only as a counterpoint to those in 4-year institutions. Rather, the contrasts presented here should be viewed as (a) evidence that these educationally effective practices are composed to meet unique needs of the institutions in the 2-year sector and (b) as a guide to filter the predominant literature base on FYSs to allow community college practitioners and scholars to implement and define this kind of intervention on their own terms. To that end, this section spotlights features of the FYS pertaining to the purpose of the seminar and characteristics of how these courses are structured on campuses.

Figure 5.1.   Comparison of Type of Primary First-Year Seminar on Campus by Institution Type (2-Year $n = 200$, 4-Year $n = 586$)

	EO	A-UC	A-VT	PP-D	BSS	HY	Other
■ Two-year	54.0%	20.5%	3.0%	2.0%	11.5%	8.5%	0.5%
■ Four-year	34.0%	18.4%	24.7%	4.4%	1.4%	16.0%	1.0%

EO = extended orientation, A-UC = academic seminar with uniform content, A-VT = academic seminar on various topics, PP-D = preprofessional or discipline linked, BSS = basic study skills, HY = hybrid.
$p < .001$

Purpose of the FYS.   When taken together, several of the features of the FYS point to the purpose of the seminar in the community college context. These features include seminar type, the course objectives, course topics, and students being served.

Following a typology developed by Barefoot (1992), seminars fall into one of the following categories: (a) extended orientation, (b) academic seminar with uniform content, (c) academic seminar on various topics, (d) preprofessional or discipline linked, or (d) basic study skills. This typology was expanded in 2006 to include a sixth type, hybrid, in recognition that many institutions were combining aspects of different types of courses. See Young and Hopp (2014) for definitions and current distributions of seminar types. Knowing about the type of seminar can reveal more information about the implicit purpose of the FYS.

Respondents to the NSFYS self-identified the type(s) of FYSs present on their campuses based on definitions provided in the questionnaire (see Young & Hopp, 2014). Results show that the most common type of seminar offered at community colleges was the extended orientation course (54%). Further, as demonstrated in Figure 5.1, 2-year campuses offered extended orientation seminars and basic study skills seminars at significantly higher rates than in 4-year institutions. Conversely, 4-year institutions offer hybrid and academic seminars on various topics at higher rates than their community college counterparts.

To gather information about the purpose of the FYS on community college campuses, respondents to the NSFYS were asked to identify the most important course objectives for the FYS. Several objectives were commonly named by both community and 4-year institutions, such as developing a connection to the institution (44.7% 2-year; 45.0% 4-year), developing academic skills, (37.8% 2-year; 35.8% 4-year), and providing an orientation to campus resources (47.9% 2-year; 34.6% 4-year). Objectives more often named by 4-year institutions included developing critical thinking skills (14.4% 2-year; 26.2% 4-year) and creating a common first-year experience (16.0% 2-year; 23.4% 4-year). However, some more frequently reported course objectives for FYS in community colleges were developing study skills (44.7% 2-year; 11.9% 4-year) and self-exploration or personal development (26.6% 2-year; 13.8% 4-year). These objectives highlight an important role of the FYS in supporting students entering community colleges who may come from a variety of backgrounds and levels of preparation. However, it is not enough to understand the institution's stated purpose for the FYS. Understanding the format by which institutions deliver on those objectives can also provide a useful insight into the implicit purpose of the seminar.

When respondents were asked to identify the most common course topics for the FYS, participants from community colleges listed study skills (50.5%), campus resources (47.9%), and academic planning or advising (44.7%). These objectives and topics are in alignment with the type of seminar being offered. In aggregate, these features of the FYS suggest community colleges use these courses to orient students to support services on campus and to develop critical academic skills required to be successful in college.

Respondents reported most frequently that seminars on community college campuses were more often aimed at academically underprepared students (28.0%), students enrolled in developmental education courses (20.7%), and students within specific majors (13.3%). Approximately 4 in 10 (42.7%) 2-year institutions reported requiring all first-year students enroll in the FYS compared to three quarters (75.2%) of 4-year campuses. This suggests that community colleges have adopted a more targeted approach focusing the seminar as an intervention for those entering students at the greatest risk of attrition.

The purpose of FYS in community college contexts appear to focus on meeting the needs of the diversity of students entering these open access institutions. Although fewer 2-year institutions than 4-year institutions require all students to enroll in a FYS, they have more specific student populations who are required to enroll. The results from the NSFYS suggest community colleges are taking a made-to-measure approach in the FYS—finding an established pattern for success that applies to their students and applying it selectively as opposed to broadly.

Course Structure.   One key mechanism for delivering on the promise of the FYS is the structure of the course itself. Understanding aspects of the course such as the number of students in each section, whether the course

Figure 5.2.   Comparison of Approximate Class Size for First-Year Seminar Sections by Institution Type (2-Year $n = 194$, 4-Year $n = 583$)

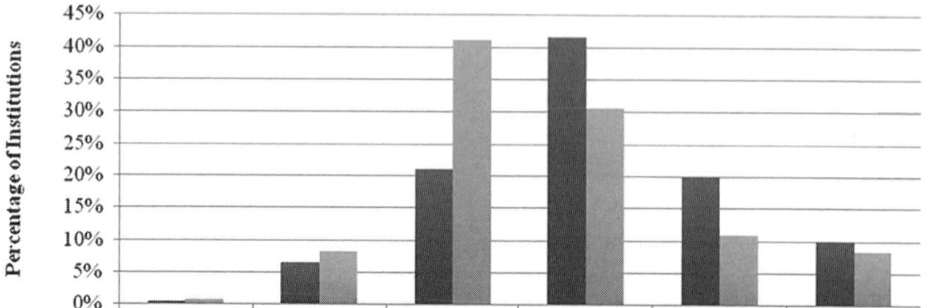

	<10	10–14	15–19	20–24	25–29	30 or more
■Two-year	0.5%	6.5%	21.1%	41.7%	20.1%	10.1%
■Four-year	0.7%	8.2%	41.1%	30.7%	11.0%	8.4%

Approximate Class Size for Each Section

$p < .001$

is offered for credit and how those credits are applied, and the incorporation of online components provides insight into how these educational environments are created and maintained at community colleges.

An important structural feature that describes the educational environment is the number of students enrolled in each section. To be able to provide attention to students' varied needs and to create community, FYS have historically been smaller, with increased pressure to bring enrollment below 20 students per section (Hunter & Linder, 2005; Young & Hopp, 2014). As demonstrated in Figure 5.2, 28.1% of community colleges report class sizes of approximately 19 students or fewer, yet a majority of responding campuses (69.8%) report class sizes less than or equal to 24 students. Conversely, nearly a third (30.2%) report 25 or more students in each section. Compared to 4-year institutions, class sizes are larger at 2-year campuses (see Figure 5.2).

Responses to the NSFYS suggest that community college campuses acknowledge the benefits of the FYS and recognize this value in the form of awarding academic credit for the seminar: the course carries credit at 93.2% of community colleges. Most 2-year institutions (46.6%) reported offering the FYS as a one-credit course, although a substantial proportion (40.9%) of community colleges indicated the seminar carries three credits. The differences between 2- and 4-year institutions are minor in the awarding of and the amount of credit for the FYS. Yet, noteworthy differences exist between 2- and 4-year campuses as to how those credits are applied. Community college campuses more frequently assign credit as electives (59.1% 2-year; 31.1% 4-year) or major requirements (11.4% 2-year; 7.5% 4-year) than 4-year campuses, whereas 4-year campuses more frequently grant FYS credit

NEW DIRECTIONS FOR COMMUNITY COLLEGES • DOI: 10.1002/cc

as a completion of general education requirements (38.6% 2-year; 65.1% 4-year).

An additional structural feature that is worthy of note is the use of online technology in the FYS to deliver course content. Community colleges more frequently reported incorporating online components (79.9%) in their FYS than did 4-year institutions (53.1%). Moreover, community colleges also more frequently reported offering online-only sections of the course (59.6%) than 4-year colleges and universities (16.1%). The use of online tools can provide an amount of support at a distance and in an asynchronous manner that do not require the delivery of the benefits to the student to be bound by place and time. However, the development of community, one of the core areas of impact for FYSs, may suffer in a virtual learning environment.

Important lessons about the FYS in community colleges can be learned from the results related to course structure. First, based on the figures related to the relatively small class size and the awarding of credit, community colleges are investing resources in this HIP. Second, 2-year institutions are more frequently using online tools to provide the benefits of the FYS to their students. This signals a commitment of these institutions to become flexible to meet the needs of the students. Finally, in a related vein to the information about the purpose of the seminar, the assignment of course credits as an elective course signals the approach of the majority of community colleges as targeting the FYS to certain student populations who are at risk or in need of transition assistance; on the other hand, including it as a general education requirement communicates a desire for all students to engage in the seminar.

High-Impact Practices.   The 2012–2013 NSFYS included a focus on HIPs intentionally included in or connected to the FYS. This included seven of the remaining nine HIPs as named by AAC&U: (a) writing-intensive experiences in the FYS, (b) collaboration and teamwork, (c) diversity and global learning, (d) service learning, (e) learning communities, (f) common reading experience (as a common intellectual experience), and (g) undergraduate research. The other two HIPs (internships and senior capstone experiences) were not included as they are historically or by definition experiences that occur outside the first year.

HIPs were widely connected or integrated into FYS, as 62.8% of community colleges reported having two or more HIPs intentionally connected to the course. As the FYS is also a HIP itself, this indicates that if students engage in a seminar, on average, they have the opportunity to be exposed to three high-impact educational activities in the first year of college. The HIPs that were most frequently included or connected to the FYS in community colleges included collaborative assignments and projects (70.2%), diversity or global learning (46.8%), and learning communities (32.8%). Given that Kuh (2008) identifies engagement in at least two HIPs as a means to "enhance student engagement and increase student success" (p. 19), FYSs are an important vehicle for meeting this metric of quality in the undergraduate experience, particularly for community colleges where the timeline is more compressed for delivery of high-impact educational experiences.

As noted previously, FYS have been identified as a hub or key delivery point for important first-year student success programs. Hatch and Bohlig (2016) described this as a "hybridization" of student success activities that "blurs the conceptual lines" (p. 6) between the FYS and other HIPs on campuses. This hybridization portends well for increased benefits for those students who engage in HIPs integrated to the FYS (Finley & McNair, 2013).

Implications

As higher education professionals create, adapt, and implement FYSs on community college campuses, the question of how they can be structured to maximize the benefits for the students must remain paramount. Currently, it appears the majority of community colleges are requiring FYSs for targeted student populations, namely those who stand to benefit the most from the seminar. Students enter with a great deal of variation in ability, goals, resources (e.g., time, money, motivation, and college knowledge). Thus, as first-year programs grow on community college campuses, interested parties must consider whether it makes sense to have an institution-wide policy where one kind of seminar is set up for most or all students or whether the tide of growth must be stemmed in the interest of providing a high-quality educational environment for intentionally selected groups of students. Moreover, community colleges need multiple approaches to meet the needs of all of their different students, which suggests that more than one type of FYS may be needed.

National survey results suggest that community colleges are leveraging the FYS as a place where students have connections to other HIPs. The benefits of hybridization of student success initiatives have been demonstrated. However, careful thought must be given when these practices are combined. The benefits of combining HIPs and FYS are realized when the combined efforts are thoughtfully created, well implemented, and continually evaluated (Kuh, 2008; Young & Hopp, 2014). Thus, it is important to embed quality metrics and assessment plans into FYS programs.

These results portray the national picture of the FYS as an important and adaptive part of a wider experience aimed at supporting first-year students transitioning into community colleges. This allows practitioners to identify promising HIPs, but more needs to be known about how and why these environments are so powerful, especially among community college students. However, research on the benefits of FYSs remains focused on 4-year colleges and universities (see Brownell & Swaner, 2010; Griffin & Romm, 2008; Porter & Swing, 2006). The contrasts we presented between 2- and 4-year institutions revealed unique purposes and structures of the FYS in 2-year colleges. It is now time for community college scholars and practitioners to further the conversation about what it means to adapt, recreate, and question the assumptions underlying the FYS in the 2-year sector. More needs to be known about what happens in the educational transaction in HIPs in the first year, such as FYS, that lead to positive outcomes, especially among students in community college contexts. The more we can learn about how particular features of the educational environment lead to improved educational outcomes for students, the more effective we can be at delivering on the promise of higher education in the United States.

References

ACT. (2014). *2014 retention/completion summary tables.* Iowa City, IA: Author.

Barefoot, B. O. (1992). *Helping first-year college students climb the academic ladder: Report of a national survey of freshman seminar programming in American higher education* (Unpublished doctoral dissertation). College of William and Mary, Williamsburg, VA.

Barefoot, B. O., & Fidler, P. P. (1996). *The 1994 National Survey of Freshman Seminar programs: Continuing innovation in the collegiate curriculum.* Columbia, SC: University of South Carolina, National Resource Center for The First-Year Experience and Students in Transition.

Boggs, G. R. (2011). The American community college: From access to success. In T. Brown, M. C. King, & P. Stanley (Eds.), *Fulfilling the promise of the community college: Increasing first-year student engagement and success* (Monograph No. 56, pp. 3–14). Columbia, SC: University of South Carolina, National Resource Center for The First-Year Experience and Students in Transition.

Brownell, J. A., & Swaner, L. E. (2010). *Five high-impact practices: Research on learning outcomes, completion, and quality.* Washington, DC: Association of American Colleges and Universities.

Center for Community College Student Engagement (CCCSE). (2012). *A matter of degrees: Promising practices for community college student success: A first look.* Austin, TX: The University of Texas at Austin, Community College Leadership Program.

Center for Community College Student Engagement (CCCSE). (2015). *Survey results for 2014 Survey of Entering College Students (SENSE).* Austin, TX: The University of Texas at Austin, Community College Leadership Program.

Cohen, A. M., & Brawer, F. B. (1996). *The American community college* (3rd ed.). San Francisco, CA: Jossey-Bass.

Cohen, A. M., & Kisker, C. B. (2010). *American higher education: Emergence and growth of the contemporary system* (2nd ed.). San Francisco, CA: Jossey-Bass.

Finley, A., & McNair, T. B. (2013). *Assessing underserved students' engagement in high-impact practices.* Washington, DC: Association of American Colleges & Universities.

Gahagan, J. S. (2002). *A historical and theoretical framework for the first-year seminar: A brief history. The 2000 National Survey of First-Year Seminar Programs: Continuing innovations in the collegiate curriculum* (Monograph No. 35, pp. 11–76). Columbia, SC: University of South Carolina, National Resource Center for The First-Year Experience and Students in Transition.

Gordon, V. P. (1989). Origins and purposes of the freshman seminar. In M. L. Upcraft, J. N. Gardner, & Associates (Eds.), *The freshman year experience.* San Francisco, CA: Jossey-Bass.

Greenfield, G. M., Keup, J. R., & Gardner, J. N. (2013). *Developing and sustaining successful first-year programs: A guide for practitioners.* San Francisco, CA: Jossey-Bass.

Griffin, A. M., & Romm, J. (2008). *Exploring the evidence: Reporting research on first-year seminars* (Vol. IV). Columbia, SC: University of South Carolina, National Resource Center for The First-Year Experience and Students in Transition.

Habley, W. R. (2011). Enhancing first-year success in the community college: What works in student retention. In T. Brown, M. C. King, & P. Stanley (Eds.), *Fulfilling the promise of the community college: Increasing first-year student engagement and success* (Monograph No. 56, pp. 34–49). Columbia, SC: University of South Carolina, National Resource Center for The First-Year Experience and Students in Transition.

Hatch, D. K., & Bohlig, E. M. (2016). An empirical typology of the latent programmatic structure of promising practices at community colleges. *Research in Higher Education, 57*(1), 72–98. doi:10.1007/s11162-015-9379-6

Hunter, M. S., & Linder, C. W. (2005). First-year seminars. In M. L. Upcraft, J. N. Gardner, B. O. Barefoot, & Associates (Eds.), *Challenging and supporting the first-year student* (pp. 275–291). San Francisco, CA: Jossey-Bass.

Karp, M. M., Bickierstaff, S., Rucks-Ahidiana, Z., Bork, R. H., Barragan, M., & Edgecombe, N. (2012). *College 101 courses for applied learning and student success* (Working Paper No. 49). New York, NY: Columbia University, Teachers College, Community College Research Center.

Koch, S. S., Griffin, B. Q., & Barefoot, B. O. (2014). *National Survey of Student Success Initiatives at Two-Year Colleges.* Brevard, NC: John N. Gardner Institute for Excellence in Undergraduate Education.

Kuh, G. D. (2008). *High-impact educational practices: What they are, who has access to them, and why they matter.* Washington, DC: Association of American Colleges and Universities.

McClenney, K. (2011). Understanding entering community college students: Learning from student voices. In T. Brown, M. C. King, & P. Stanley (Eds.), *Fulfilling the promise of the community college: Increasing first-year student engagement and success* (Monograph No. 56, pp. 15–34). Columbia, SC: University of South Carolina, National Resource Center for The First-Year Experience and Students in Transition.

Padgett, R. D., & Keup, J. R. (2011). *2009 National Survey of First-Year Seminars: Ongoing efforts t support students in transition* (Research Reports on College Transitions, No. 2). Columbia, SC: University of South Carolina, National Resource Center for The First-Year Experience and Students in Transition.

Padgett, R. D., Keup, J. R., & Pascarella, E. T. (2013). The impact of first-year seminars on college students' life-long learning orientations. *Journal of Student Affairs Research and Practice, 50*(2), 133–151.

Pascarella, E. T., & Terenzini, P. T. (2005). *How college affects students: A third decade of research.* San Francisco, CA: Jossey-Bass.

Porter, S. R., & Swing, R. L. (2006). Understanding how first-year seminars affect persistence. *Research in Higher Education, 47*(1), 89–109.

Schneider, C. G., & Albertine, S. (2013). Introduction. In A. Finley & T. McNair (Eds.), *Assessing underserved students' engagement in high-impact practices* (pp. v–vii). Washington, DC: Association of American Colleges & Universities.

Swing, R. L. (2002). *Series of essays on the First-Year Initiative Benchmarking Study.* Brevard, NC: Policy Center on the First-Year of College. Retrieved from http://www.sc.edu/fye/resources/assessment/essays/Swing-8.28.02.html

Tobolowsky, B. F., (2005). *The 2003 National Survey on First-Year Seminars: Continuing innovations in the collegiate curriculum* (Monograph No. 41). Columbia, SC: University of South Carolina, National Resource Center for The First-Year Experience and Students in Transition.

Tobolowsky, B. F., & Associates (2008). *2006 National Survey of First-Year Seminars: Continuing innovations in the collegiate curriculum* (Monograph No. 51). Columbia, SC: University of South Carolina, National Resource Center for The First-Year Experience and Students in Transition.

Tobolowsky, B. F., Cox, B. E., & Wagner, M. T. (2005). *Exploring the evidence: Reporting research on first-year seminars, Volume III* (Monograph No. 42). Columbia, SC:

National Resource Center for The First-Year Experience and Students in Transition, University of South Carolina.

Young, D. G., & Hopp, J. M. (2014). *2012–2013 National Survey of First-Year Seminars: Exploring high-impact practices in the first college year* (Research Report No. 4). Columbia, SC: University of South Carolina, National Resource Center for The First-Year Experience & Students in Transition.

Dallin George Young is the assistant director for research, grants, and assessment at the National Resource Center for The First-Year Experience and Students in Transition, University of South Carolina.

Jennifer R. Keup is the director of the National Resource Center for The First-Year Experience and Students in Transition and an affiliated faculty member in the Department of Educational Leadership and Policies in the College of Education at the University of South Carolina.

6

This chapter examines community college first-year experience programs using critical race theory and ecological theory. The study draws on diverse students' experiences with access, support, and long-term success within community colleges to assess how these programs foster student success, as told through the voices of student participants.

Community College First-Year Experience Programs: Examining Student Access, Experience, and Success from the Student Perspective

Nancy Acevedo-Gil, Desiree D. Zerquera

Although the majority of community college students enter with aspirations of earning a college degree, completion rates are dismal (Moore & Shulock, 2010). Student success programs have received increased attention as a key institutional resource used to improve outcomes (Center for Community College Student Engagement, 2012; Schnell & Doetkott, 2003). Although attention has been given to programmatic interventions during the first year (Hankin & Gardner, 1996; Tinto, 1999), more work has argued that these efforts targeting students during their first semesters in college are just one intervention encapsulating a set of practices aimed at supporting students (Karp, Chapter 3; Young & Keup, Chapter 5).

Despite noting the significance of these programs, previous literature has failed to reflect the voices of students who participate in them. This chapter provides insight into the student experiences, by employing an analysis of a community college first-year experience (FYE) program. To do so, this chapter uses data from interviews held with community college students who participated in an FYE program that provided individualized counseling, supplemental instruction, and cohort-based classes, with the aim of improving student preparation, retention, and transfer. The student insights are valuable for campus leaders when considering approaches to support and sustain community college student success. The following questions guided the study:

NEW DIRECTIONS FOR COMMUNITY COLLEGES, no. 175, Fall 2016 © 2016 Wiley Periodicals, Inc.
Published online in Wiley Online Library (wileyonlinelibrary.com) • DOI: 10.1002/cc.20213

1. Why do students participate in FYE?
2. How does FYE support students' transitions to and experiences in community college?
3. How does FYE prepare students to succeed beyond the first year of college?

Overview of Relevant Literature

Community colleges serve high proportions of students from marginalized backgrounds (i.e., students of color and those from low-income backgrounds) (National Center for Public Policy and Higher Education, 2011). Success rates are disparaging, as only 39% of degree-seeking community college students complete a degree or certificate within 6 years—less than any other institutional pathway (Shapiro, Dundar, Yuan, Harrell, & Wakhungu, 2014). To address attainment gaps, research highlights how programs can support student success.

Supporting Marginalized Students at Community Colleges.   Retention, completion, and transfer rates are lower for marginalized students than White and more affluent counterparts (Dougherty & Kienzl, 2006; National Center for Education Statistics, 2015). Studies attribute trends to differential resources available in secondary schools that serve high populations of marginalized students (Rogers et al., 2010) and high placement rates into developmental education trajectories that delay success (Crisp & Delgado, 2014). Community colleges themselves have been critiqued as being designed to discourage students from transferring (Brint & Karabel, 1989) and better serving students from more privileged backgrounds (Jain, Herrera, Bernal, & Solórzano, 2011; Walker, Pearson, & Murrell, 2010). Research has focused on identifying programs and practices to support community college students and address these impediments.

First-Year Experience Programs.   Previous studies note the importance of the first year of college on student success and emphasize the positive role of first-year programs for college transition (Pascarella & Terenzini, 2005). These programs vary widely and typically include academic and social resources (Hatch & Bohlig, 2016). Academic programs that promote community college student success have dedicated faculty, emphasize access and excellence, have a unique culture that fosters cohesion, and provide academic advising (Nitecki, 2011). Other typical elements of FYE that have been found to influence student success positively include learning communities (Scrivener et al., 2008), study skills courses (Windham, Rehfuss, Williams, Pugh, & Tincher-Ladner, 2014) and student support programs (Fike & Fike, 2008). However, the majority of research on FYE programs has been quantitative and does not include the student voice. This chapter centers the experiences of community college students within FYE programs and their experiences with transition and success.

New Directions for Community Colleges • DOI: 10.1002/cc

Conceptual Frameworks

In this chapter, we apply Bronfenbrenner's ecological perspective (1979, 2005) through a critical race theory in education (CRTE) (Solórzano, 1998) lens to understand the experiences of marginalized community college students within FYE programs.

Ecological Theory.   Bronfenbrenner (1979, 2005) offers a model of ecological development, which considers the interrelationships between an individual, their own traits and context. The perspective focuses on the effects of different environmental contexts, from an individual's direct environment to the social, cultural, and historical contexts they engage. Bronfenbrenner notes the influence of *proximal processes*—patterns of interaction between an individual and their microsystem—to highlight the importance of interactions and support from within the immediate environment.

This lens helps consider students' experiences in ways that foreground the interplay between personal characteristics and factors within the environment. The implications highlight, as captured by Ozaki and Renn (2015), that "two people from the same background may experience an environment very differently and two people from very different backgrounds may have similar experiences in the environment" (p. 96). Although this study does not allow us to examine the multiple systems that students engage with, it provides us a lens through which to consider the various resources and constraints that students experience when navigating community college programs intended to support them. We combine this view with a critical perspective not merely to accept students' descriptions of their experiences but to challenge the system that shapes them.

Critical Race Theory in Education (CRTE).   CRTE provides a social-justice lens to examine the educational experiences, conditions, and outcomes of marginalized students (Smith-Maddox & Solórzano, 2002) and identify and challenge dominant ideologies and systemic inequities in education (Solórzano, 1998). Solórzano (1998) identifies five tenets of CRTE that guide the research process and that are incorporated into the approach of this work: centrality and intersectionality of race/racism with other forms of subordination, challenge to dominant ideology, commitment to social justice, centrality of experiential knowledge of People of Color, and an interdisciplinary perspective. Jain (2010) argues for community college research to include CRTE as a lens because the sector serves a majority of students of color and the outcomes for marginalized students at community colleges are dismal.

Data Methods and Study Context

Data for this study derived from the larger Pathways to Postsecondary Success study (Solórzano, Datnow, Park, & Watford, 2013), a 5-year, multi-method project that examined postsecondary trajectories of low-income

NEW DIRECTIONS FOR COMMUNITY COLLEGES • DOI: 10.1002/cc

community college students. Between December 2010 and September 2012, the Pathways research team conducted three waves of semistructured interviews with 110 low-income students at three different community colleges in southern California. Pathways researchers coded the data using deductive and inductive coding (Fereday & Muir-Cochrane, 2008), resulting in seven code families and 43 codes.

For this chapter, we analyzed the interview data deductively from the "Honors Transfer Program" code within the "Academics" code family, which included all FYE participants. Participants in FYE were from one community college. Of these 42 participants, 24 participated in FYE and shared their experiences with information transmittal, the transfer process, and interactions with an advisor. All 24 participants were from low-income backgrounds; 13 identified as Latina/o, 5 as African American, 5 as Asian American, and 1 student as mixed; 9 were male and 15 female. At the college, FYE served as a comprehensive program that aimed to improve student preparation, retention, and transfer for first-year students who placed into developmental courses. The program staff consisted of a combination of counselors, academic coaches, supplemental instructors, and faculty liaisons.

Findings

Our analysis of findings centered on examining participants' initial enrollment in FYE, experiences within the program, and preparation to succeed. We highlight the recurring accounts of support and challenges encountered by students and discuss these themes next.

Choosing to Participate in FYE.   Overwhelmingly, participants discussed their purpose for enrolling in FYE as motivated by family members and peers who attended community college and insisted that FYE was essential in was an essential resource to achieve academic goals. As Ariana recalled, "My brother advised me to join FYE." Participants learned about the benefits of FYE from personal and familial networks that benefitted from the program, suggesting the positive impacts of the program. In turn, after experiencing a supportive environment, the participants then referred future generations into FYE. As captured by Natalia: "I always tell my little cousins...'definitely go to FYE. Please, I'm begging you, go to FYE. It's the best thing you could ever do at a community college.'" The participants noted the benefits of enrolling in FYE and aimed to share the wealth of resources with future college students.

Facilitating a Successful Community College Transition.   The participants explained that enrolling in FYE provided access to various institutional resources and supported a successful academic and social transition. In particular, the wealth of FYE resources that facilitated the transition into college included learning community courses, tutors within classrooms, and assigned advisors.

New Directions for Community Colleges • DOI: 10.1002/cc

A number of participants discussed the significant role of the FYE peer community in facilitating the transition to college. Catherine elaborated on the transition:

> I was like, "I don't know how I'm gonna deal with this," or "How am I gonna deal with the teachers?" ... But it was really helpful to find FYE ... I liked it because I was able to be with the same people for the first year, and now I have friends, so it made it really easy to transfer in and to get adjusted to school, which was nice.

As captured by her experience and echoed in others' accounts, the learning community facilitated a peer network and supported adjustment to college.

Academic resources, such as in-class tutors in select FYE courses, were also described as being valuable in students' academic success. In describing the role of in-class tutors, Catherine noted: "It helps, because if the teacher is really busy and you have a simple question, they can answer it ... [they] have information that you don't hear about around campus, and they can tell you, and then you can go find (it)." As suggested here, the tutors provided more than just curriculum-specific academic support; they also connected students with other resources.

One key resource that participants emphasized throughout the interviews was access to FYE advisors. The participants had trusting relationships with the FYE advisors and staff, who provided individual academic guidance. Natalia exemplified the process:

> It's easier knowing that I could just come to an office where they already know me ... Everybody else has to go downstairs to all the other counselors. You get a different advisor every time ... but here I have my own (advisor)—they know my story. They know me personally. They've seen me cry.

As captured by Natalia's experience, access to an academic coach not only facilitated the information-seeking process but also entailed personalized guidance. Echoing similar sentiments, another participant explained the importance of an advisor knowing a student's background, which established a trusting guidance relationship.

In addition to the academic and social support provided by advisors, participants described their role in providing validation and encouragement to pursue academic goals. As exemplified by Ariana: "[FYE advisors and staff] encourage you, 'No, no, stay onto what your plans are. Keep following your goals. Stick to your goals. Do what it takes for you to be in it.'" In this excerpt, the participant depicted the messages communicated by FYE institutional agents, which were contextualized as diminishing self-doubt and reaffirming her presence in college. Many participants conveyed similar sentiments; the majority discussed the access to academic advising resources as being part of the privileges for FYE students. Moreover, participants highly valued the resources when transitioning to college.

Success Beyond the First Year.   Participants also described enrollment in FYE as promoting success along the transfer pathway, with peer networks, faculty, and counseling courses providing key navigation skills and information. For instance, participants described ways in which they built on their peer networks and the practices within FYE courses to develop academic support structures in non-FYE courses. Eric recalled, "We created a group of us... you form groups to study to get through a course." This demonstrated how the impact of FYE extended beyond the core classes to apply academic skills in future courses.

Moreover, students described pedagogical practices that FYE instructors used, which were instrumental to academic success. As Danielle explained,

> You grow a relationship with [FYE teachers]... I've been able to go to them with questions and they have answers–if I don't understand it, they're willing to explain it to me... When I got out of the cohorts and started going to other classes and dealing with other teachers, I took that and was willing to go up to other teachers and ask them questions and go to their office hours... it made me feel like they were willing to help me, not just teaching.

As reflected by participants, FYE instructors were approachable and responsive to student concerns through various pedagogical practices. The teaching approaches resulted in students resituating their understanding of faculty members' roles within higher education, developing institutional trust and the confidence needed to address future instructors.

FYE students also took required counseling courses, which they cited widely and described as being particularly helpful. The required courses included introduction to college and career planning. As Jason explained,

> I know a little more than other students ... [the FYE class] touched on different subjects that college students battle with. Sometimes I talk to people or people tell me about their children in community college and they're like, "They don't know what to do"... It's like, "Okay. Do they have this? Do they have that?" And it's like, "Oh, no."

Although describing the counseling courses, this participant exemplified a point that all FYE students noted during their second interview: FYE increased the knowledge to navigate community college. In the required counseling courses, the participants learned about and gained confidence on how to navigate likely obstacles they would encounter as a student, while being aware of the greater challenges they might have faced had they not enrolled in FYE.

Institutional Obstacles. Despite the benefits of being in FYE, participants faced challenges within the institution. For instance, participants recounted obstacles that resulted from a lack of guidance with processes that occurred before enrollment, such as placement exams and financial aid applications. Tanya elaborated on her experience that resulted from receiving misguidance from a community college outreach counselor who visited her high school:

> When I was getting in the (FYE) program . . . [my FYE counselor] asked me about my scores. She told me to place again so I could try to get into [college-level] English . . . I explained to her, . . . "this one counselor that went to my (high) school told me not to try hard" . . . (My counselor) was like, "She gave you wrong advice." . . . that's when I started understanding everything . . . the lower you place, the longer you are gonna be here . . . So then I was like, "Okay, I'm gonna really try." I was one point away [from college-level English]. So, she was like, "I'll waive it."

As Tanya exemplified, the misguidance provided by an outreach counselor, combined with the lack of institutional resources to support students through these processes, resulted in what participants described as being uninformed and misinformed. Although FYE was able to support Tanya other participants dealt with long-term implications and limitations due to misinformation. For example, a participant who was uninformed did not take placement exams and as a result could not enroll in math or English courses. Similarly, other participants discussed limitations that they experienced when it came to misinformation about the financial aid process, which resulted in delayed and/or nonexistent financial aid awards.

Further, although the participants valued strengthening skills to navigate college and continual access to FYE advisors, the lack of institutional resources created challenges, particularly during the transfer process. For example, participants described the inaccessibility of counselors, which made it difficult to obtain information about specific major requirements. Concurrently, participants recounted a lack of support in making decisions about their future. Natalia captured what others shared and exemplified that an FYE student could remain in a state of limbo due to the aforementioned dilemmas:

> I'm always thinking, "Should I just get an AA—settle with that?" I don't wanna settle, but I'm thinking I have to . . . it's been such a headache for me trying to think of what I wanna do in these last couple weeks because my registration was coming up, and then I'm thinking, "Where am I gonna go after this? I can't go to a big old UCLA, USC." I was looking at schools out of state, and I was just doing a lot of research, so now my head is filled with stuff, and I really don't know what I'm gonna do.

NEW DIRECTIONS FOR COMMUNITY COLLEGES • DOI: 10.1002/cc

Despite being actively involved in FYE, Natalia revealed an uncertainty about her postsecondary pathway choices, highlighting a lack of confidence and outstanding questions about how best to continue in her academic endeavors. However, the FYE resources did not always allow participants to address such uncertainties. Thus, when participants had concerns that required more in-depth counseling, FYE resources did not suffice. Notably, several students expressed these sentiments during interview two, in contrast to the general sense of certainty conveyed in the first interview.

Discussion of Findings

The findings from this study focus on the experiences of community college students in a FYE program, highlighting access to the program, the perceived short- and long-term benefits, and the institutional barriers that inhibited students' success. Through the lens of our ecological and CRTE framework, we consider the findings in light of the literature on community college FYE programs.

Many of our findings point to the value of promising and high-impact programs and practices discussed throughout the other articles presented in this special issue. The voices of the participants show *how* these elements, within the context of a FYE program, mattered for their success. Findings reveal that when it comes to programmatic elements and institutional practices, the whole is greater than the sum of each of the individual parts. Participants' experiences reveal how each individual resource or practice reflected in student success program research was not singularly sufficient but created a synergistic support system for students. For instance, students' long-term success in non-FYE courses relied on not just the support of faculty in the FYE courses to teach valuable navigational skills but a cohort of peers and the course content itself, all of which students referred to in accounts of their experiences. This finding speaks to previous work and potentially explains why the effects of programs, such as FYE, diminish over time (Scrivener et al., 2008; Weiss et al., 2014).

This example also highlights the significance of proximal processes where participants perceived the most positive impacts as peers, advisors, and faculty created a holistic support system surrounding students. This echoes previous work by Yosso (2005) and others who establish that individuals from communities of color draw from personal networks to succeed in education. However, although family and peers played an important role in students' access to FYE in particular, the manner in which participants discussed the roles of others within their immediate environment at the institution demonstrates the ongoing importance of personal connections. As low-income students of color, participants created a community within FYE, highlighting the importance of supportive peers and institutional agents within students' immediate environment.

Despite the positive influence of the FYE community, there were influences at play from the broader environment of the community college.

NEW DIRECTIONS FOR COMMUNITY COLLEGES • DOI: 10.1002/cc

Although FYE provided support to combat traditional community college barriers, the participants highlighted various barriers that non-FYE students experienced and FYE students faced after their participation in the program concluded. For instance, the participants highlighted the significance of access to advisors that FYE enrollment provided, drawing direct comparisons to non-FYE students who had more limited access to advisors. This finding speaks to the notion of mechanisms of nonacademic support distributed to all students throughout college (Karp, Chapter 3). Although the community college sector increases college access for students of marginalized backgrounds, the sector is greatly underfunded and receives less state financial support than other sectors but is charged to serve the most disenfranchised students (Hendrick, Hightower, & Gregory, 2006; Mullin, 2010). Though boutique programs, such as FYE, foster student success, they enroll only a small percentage of eligible students. Without adequate funding and appropriate resource allocation that equitably considers the support needed, institutional policies and practices will continue to exclude thousands of low-income students and students of color from educational opportunities. These trends highlight the impact of the context of students' educational experience, from within their immediate institution to the politics of the state. More can and should be done to provide equitable educational resources to all students aspiring to transfer.

Recommendations for Community College Practitioners and Policy Makers

We provide three recommendations for community college policy makers and practitioners. First, the most urgent recommendation is to enhance availability and quality of advising. Community college advisors face unmanageable caseloads, with the implications exemplified in the findings here. Although FYE students benefited from having access to an assigned advisor, findings revealed institutional barriers such as lack of access to dependable advising outside of FYE. An increase in the number of advisors would benefit *all* students.

Given resource constraints in community colleges and the benefits of peer networks, institutions may think creatively outside of formal, full-time professional staff. For instance, 4-year college students who transferred from a similar 2-year institution may supplement advising staff via work-study positions, as modeled by Americorps College Advising Corps and TRiO programs at 4-year colleges, which hire college students to guide high school students with college preparation. Small-group advising during critical times in the academic calendar and faculty advising are other recommendations that would enhance availability, build on peer networks, and support students' connection to the institution.

Further, the way advising is provided is equally important. Advisors should work from an asset-based philosophy and participate in professional development opportunities to understand how to counter deficit ideologies that may pervade community colleges. Findings emphasize the role of advisors' high expectations and encouragement to influence students' success and the detrimental impacts of misinformation communicated to students. We recommend that institutions provide professional development opportunities for their advisors that foster staff that cultivate high aspirations and expectations of students and who are grounded in community cultural wealth frameworks (Yosso, 2005).

Second, we recommend that community colleges offer courses that teach college navigational skills and foster student communities. Leaders should develop policies to require or encourage first-year students to participate in these courses, for example, by incorporating such a course into general education requirements for all degrees. These courses can be designed to also facilitate a learning community among students and foster supportive peer relationships.

Third, we recommend that instructors develop and maintain pedagogical practices that foster trusting relationships and support low-income students of color. These findings demonstrate the significant impact that FYE instructors had on students' success via a demonstration of care for students and being approachable and responsive to student questions. Thus, instructors should maintain an asset-based perspective and implement pedagogical practices where students ask questions as a part of the learning process and make themselves available for individual interactions with students during class time. By institutionalizing an increase in access to FYE-type benefits, colleges will reach a larger number of students and reduce the institutional barriers experienced by all community college students.

Conclusion

This chapter addresses the processes involved in the experiences of community college students and the potential of FYE programs in shaping student success. FYE programs contribute positively to student experiences but institutional barriers remain. Although the community college sector often serves to increase access to higher education, colleges must also expand student success. To maximize student success, policies must go beyond establishing accountability benchmarks and ensure an equitable distribution of educational resources and opportunities available to *all* students, such as the academic and counseling resources available in FYE programs.

Acknowledgments

This research was derived from the Pathways to Postsecondary Success study, which focused on identifying and promoting educational pathways for low-income community college students, conducted by the University of California All Campus Consortium (UC/ACCORD) on the Research for Diversity, through the generous funding of the Bill and Melinda Gates Foundation. The research findings reflect the opinion of the authors and not necessarily those of the Gates Foundation. The authors would like to thank Dr. Daniel G. Solórzano and Dr. Lluliana Alonso for their time and support with accessing the dataset.

References

Brint, S., & Karabel, J. (1989). *The diverted dream: Community colleges and the promise of educational opportunity in America,1900-1985*. New York: Oxford University Press.

Bronfenbrenner, U. (1979). *The ecology of human development: Experiments by nature and design*. Cambridge, MA: Harvard University Press.

Bronfenbrenner, U. (2005). *Making human beings human: Bioecological perspectives on human development*. Thousand Oaks, CA: Sage Publications.

Center for Community College Student Engagement. (2013). A Matter of Degrees: Engaging Practices, Engaging Students (High-Impact Practices for Community College Student Engagement). Austin, TX: The University of Texas at Austin, Community College Leadership Program.

Crisp, G., & Delgado, C. (2014). The impact of developmental education on community college persistence and vertical transfer. *Community College Review, 42*(2), 99–117. doi:10.1177/0091552113516488

Dougherty, K. J., & Kienzl, G. S. (2006). It's not enough to get through the open door: Inequalities by social background in transfer from community colleges to four-year colleges. *Teachers College Record, 108*(3), 452–487.

Fike, D. S., & Fike, R. (2008). Predictors of first-year student retention in the community college. *Community College Review, 36*(2), 68–88. doi:10.1177/0091552108320222

Fereday, J., & Muir-Cochrane, E. (2008). Demonstrating rigor using thematic analysis: A hybrid approach of inductive and deductive coding and theme development. *International Journal of Qualitative Methods, 5*(1), 80–92.

Hankin, J. N., & Gardner, J. N. (1996). The freshman year experience: A philosophy for higher education in the new millennium. In J. N. Hankin (Ed.), *The community college: Opportunity and access for America's first-year students* (Monograph No. 19, pp. 1–10). Columbia, SC: National Resource Center for The First-Year Experience and Students in Transition, University of South Carolina.

Hatch, D. K., & Bohlig, E. M. (2016). An empirical typology of the latent programmatic structure of promising practices at community colleges. *Research in Higher Education, 57*(1), 72–98. doi:10.1007/s11162-015-9379-6

Hendrick, R. Z., Hightower, W. H., & Gregory, D. E. (2006). State funding limitations and community college open door policy: Conflicting priorities? *Community College Journal of Research & Practice, 30*(8), 627–640. doi:10.1080/10668920600746078

Jain, D. (2010). Critical race theory and community colleges: Through the eyes of women student leaders of color. *Community College Journal of Research and Practice, 34*(1), 78–91. doi:10.1080/10668920903385855

Jain, D., Herrera, A., Bernal, S., & Solórzano, D. (2011). Critical race theory and the transfer function: Introducing a transfer receptive culture. *Community College Journal of Research and Practice, 35*(3), 252–266. doi:10.1080/10668926.2011.526525

Mullin, C. (2010). *Doing more with less: The inequitable funding of community colleges*. Washington, DC: American Association of Community Colleges.

Moore, C., & Shulock, N. (2010). *Divided we fail: Improving completion and closing racial gaps in california's community colleges*. Washington, DC: Institute for Higher Education Leadership & Policy.

National Center for Education Statistics. (2015). *Digest of education statistics: 2013 (NCES 2015-011)*. Washington, DC: Author.

National Center for Public Policy and Higher Education. (2011). *Affordability and transfer: Critical to increasing baccalaureate degree completion*. San Jose, CA: Author.

Nitecki, E. M. (2011). The power of the program: How the academic program can improve community college student success. *Community College Review, 39*(2), 98–120. doi:10.1177/0091552111404926

Ozaki, C. C., & Renn, K. A. (2015). Engaging multiracial college students. In S. J. Quaye & S. R. Harper (Eds.), *Student engagement in higher education: Theoretical and practical approaches for diverse populations* (2nd ed., pp. 91–104). New York, NY: Routledge.

Pascarella, E. T., & Terenzini, P.T. (2005). *How college affects students: A third decade of research* (Vol. 2). San Francisco, CA: Jossey-Bass.

Rogers, J., Fanelli, S., Freelon, R., Medina, D., Bertrand, M., & Del Razo, M. (2010). *Educational opportunities in hard times: The impact of the economic crisis on public schools and working families*. Los Angeles, CA: California Educational Opportunity Report UCLA's Institute for Democracy, Education, and Access UC All Campus Consortium on Research for Diversity.

Schnell, C. A., & Doetkott, C. D. (2003). First year seminars produce long-term impact. *Journal of College Student Retention: Research, Theory & Practice, 4*(4), 377–391.

Scrivener, S., Bloom, D., LeBlanc, A., Paxson, C., Rouse, C. E., & Sommo, C. (2008). *A good start: Two-year effects of a freshmen learning community program at Kingsborough Community College*. New York, NY: MDRC.

Shapiro, D., Dundar, A., Yuan, X., Harrell, A., & Wakhungu, P. K. (2014, November). *Completing college: A national view of student attainment rates—Fall 2008 Cohort* (Signature Report No. 8). Herndon, VA: National Student Clearinghouse Research Center.

Smith-Maddox, R., & Solórzano, D. G. (2002). Using critical theory, Paulo Freire's problem-posing method, and case study research to confront race and racism in education. *Qualitative Inquiry, 8*(1), 66–84. doi:10.1177/107780040200800105

Solórzano, D. (1998). Critical race theory, racial and gender microaggressions, and the experiences of Chicana and Chicano Scholars. *International Journal of Qualitative Studies, 11*(1), 121–136.

Solórzano, D., Datnow, A., Park, V., & Watford, T. (2013). *Pathways to postsecondary success: Maximizing opportunities for youth in poverty*. Final Report of the Pathways to Postsecondary Success Project at UC/ACCORD (All Campus Consortium on Research for Diversity). Los Angeles, CA: University of California. Retrieved from http://pathways.gseis.ucla.edu/publications/PathwaysReport.pdf

Tinto, V. (1999). Taking retention seriously: Rethinking the first year of college. *NACADA Journal, 19*(2), 5–9.

Walker, T., Pearson, F., & Murrell, P. (2010). Quality of effort and career preparation differences between African American and White community college students. *Community College Journal of Research and Practice, 34*(9), 738–754.

Weiss, M. J., Mayer, A., Cullinan, D., Ratledge, A., Sommo, C., & Diamond, J. (2014). A random assignment evaluation of learning communities at Kingsborough Community College: Seven years later. *Journal of Research on Educational Effectiveness*. doi:10.1080/19345747.2014.946634

Windham, M. H., Rehfuss, M. C., Williams, C. R., Pugh, J. V., & Tincher-Ladner, L. (2014). Retention of first-year community college students. *Community College Journal, 38*(5), 466–477. doi:10.1080/10668926.2012.743867

Yosso, T. (2005). Whose culture has capital? A critical race discussion of community cultural wealth. *Race, Ethnicity and Education, 8*(1), 69–91. doi:10.1080/1361332052000341006

Nancy Acevedo-Gil is an assistant professor in the Department of Educational Leadership and Technology at California State University, San Bernardino.

Desiree Zerquera is an assistant professor in the Department of Leadership Studies at the University of San Francisco.

New Directions for Community Colleges • DOI: 10.1002/cc

7

This chapter discusses the importance and common challenges of evaluating community college student success efforts; it includes a broad-based framework for carrying out effective evaluations.

Understanding the Effectiveness and Impact of Student Success Interventions on Campus

Bruce E. McComb, Jan W. Lyddon

How do we know an intervention or action is *high impact* or even *promising*? On what basis will an institution make a defensible judgment about the value of its efforts? It is more than guesswork and more than just measuring a series of numbers, but it is all too often left as an afterthought or relegated to the work of a (likely already overburdened) institutional research or institutional effectiveness staff to provide evidence to the effectiveness of student success initiatives. Perhaps worse yet, a practice might be considered effective because it carries a halo effect of having sponsorship from an individual or organization with considerable clout or power. If evaluation is not done well, an institution may waste resources on ineffective efforts, may fail to use formative information to improve them, and/or may fail to scale up effective ones (Berlin, 2014).

An evaluation's importance is not only for the benefit of institutional decision making. In a climate of decreasing state and federal support for higher education and increasing concerns about college affordability, community colleges are facing growing pressure to demonstrate the value of programs and interventions and justify business models with empirical evidence related to student success outcomes (e.g., completion rates, term-to-term and fall-to-fall retention, course success, and gainful employment after completion of college) (Berlin, 2014; Hess & Little, 2015). Institutions often adopt promising practices that have been developed by other colleges. Internally, community college administrators, faculty, and staff need to understand to what extent and under what conditions interventions add value and are appropriate for the college. At the same time, funders, accreditors, and those providing grants (e.g., government agencies and private

NEW DIRECTIONS FOR COMMUNITY COLLEGES, no. 175, Fall 2016 © 2016 Wiley Periodicals, Inc.
Published online in Wiley Online Library (wileyonlinelibrary.com) • DOI: 10.1002/cc.20214

foundations) are increasingly requiring the evaluation of interventions as a condition of operations.

Over the past decade, there has been a shift in interest in improving student success, not just offering access. A leading nonprofit organization in student success improvement efforts is Achieving the Dream (ATD), which is now the largest nongovernmental reform movement in higher education (www.achievingthedream.org). ATD provides participating community colleges with a variety of services including the support of two coaches, a leadership coach and a data coach. As data coaches, we help institutions develop a "culture of evidence and inquiry" that in turn supports data-informed decision making to increase student success. A key component of the culture of evidence is evaluation, demonstrating that interventions are on track to accomplish the expected outcomes (called formative evaluation) or have achieved them (summative evaluation).

This chapter draws on our combined professional experience during the past decade of coaching more than 20 institutions. There are a number of common challenges that affect institutions working to evaluate their interventions as well as a number of promising practices to address them. In the following section, we discuss some of the most common challenges we have identified from both our experience and the literature. We then offer a broad-based guide to carrying out effective evaluation of student success efforts.

Common Challenges

One of the most common challenges that affects the selection and design of interventions and their evaluation, in our experience, is the "propensity to jump quickly on a solution before fully understanding the exact problem to be solved" (Bryk, Gomez, Grunow, & LeMahieu, 2015, p. 24). College faculty and staff may be overconfident that an effort will have an expected outcome. At the core of this, we have seen numerous behaviors that are likely to interfere with good evaluation, including but not limited to an inadequate or unclear definition of the problem, a failure to develop a solid theory of change[1] to inform the selection and development of the intervention, and/or delaying the development of an evaluation plan until after the intervention is implemented.

Another challenge is that institutions sometimes focus only on large outcome measures, also known as lagging indicators (Gendron & Traub, 2015). Common lagging indicators include course success, retention[2], or completion of degrees or certificates. Although important, these outcomes are difficult to predict as they are related to student characteristics as well as numerous programs and practices already taking place on campus. Lagging indicators are like looking in the rearview mirror of a car; you can see where you have been, but you may not be able to see where you are going. Leading indicators on the other hand, are metrics that are predictive of what results are likely to be achieved and yet are often overlooked or given less attention. Leading indicators include metrics, such as attending classes, attending tutoring sessions, completing assignments on time, or participating in study groups.

Some metrics like course success can be both a leading indicator and a lagging indicator. For instance, course success is predictive of retention and completion. At the same time, as a lagging indicator, course success can often be predicted by leading indicators, such as class attendance, use of tutoring, or timely completion of assignments. By delaying evaluation to the end of the term, year, or several years, colleges are unable to understand the impacts of an intervention on leading indicators and are not able to make corrections during the course of the intervention. For evaluation purposes, exclusively using a lagging indicator, such as graduation rates or even retention rates to measure the impact of interventions such as new student orientation, is difficult at best. In the case of orientation, the extent to which students remain enrolled through the middle of the term as well as specific short-term behaviors like having a college email account set up before classes begin are likely better predictors of graduation or retention. In short, community colleges need to identify outcome measures that can be closely aligned with a particular intervention.

Community college faculty, staff, and administrators are increasingly doing more with less and are more often than not overburdened with responsibilities. This whirlwind of commitments can easily pull focus away from institutional student success goals. However, with the appropriate formative evaluation of data regarding leading indicators that are reasonably predictive of student success, colleges can maintain an ongoing focus on the intervention and make needed adjustments to maximize the impact on student success. As such, identifying and monitoring leading indicators and appropriate lagging indicators are key components of building a solid evaluation.

Some community colleges focus *only* on inputs or outputs without defining outcomes. However, community colleges engage in student success efforts in order to bring about some kind of positive change in one or more student outcomes (e.g., course success, retention/persistence, and degree completion). Outcomes must be focused, clearly defined, and measured using a methodologically rigorous research design. In our experience, colleges seldom use the gold standard for evaluation, described by MDRC President Gordon Berlin (2014) as experimental research designs that use random assignment to a treatment (i.e., a group that receives the intervention) and a control group. There are numerous intervening or extraneous variables that may have important relationships with student success outcomes (e.g., attending full time and placement in developmental education classes). Identifying as many of these variables as possible is essential in evaluating the intervention. The use of random assignment serves to control for these variables and provide a more valid measurement of the outcome.

However, using random assignment is difficult and may not always be required. Difficulties/issues in using random assignment to groups may include a random assignment process, lack of experience in using experimental design, time and effort required, sample size requirements, control of external variables, philosophical/ethical issues of random assignment, and a lack of understanding of the value of experimental research (Berlin, 2014). As an alternative, community colleges typically use a quasiexperimental design that does not require random assignment. The strength of the quasiexperimental design depends on the extent to which the comparison group is similar to the group participating in the intervention. A well-selected comparison group is a means of controlling for known extraneous variables. It is important to identify the comparison group at the onset of the intervention. Unfortunately, colleges may fail to adequately select a comparison group or so do too late. When a comparison group is not assigned prior to implementation, the college cannot ensure robust data collection on the comparison group.

Communication of the evaluation results, both formative and summative, is critically important and yet is often a challenge for evaluation teams. We advise taking care to share information with all stakeholders throughout the implementation and evaluation process and providing different types and amounts of information with different groups/stakeholders. For instance, individuals who are directly involved in implementing the intervention need detailed formative results in sufficient time to take corrective action, whereas administrators or faculty who are not directly involved may require only brief interim reports and/or a final summative report. Developing presentations and reports may require resources that are scarce (time, talent, and materials), and so communication of the evaluation is often limited to mandatory reporting. Fortunately, these challenges are not insurmountable.

Design the Evaluation While Designing the Intervention

The importance of designing the evaluation simultaneously with developing an intervention cannot be overstated. Doing so helps institutions to avoid jumping to a solution before a problem is well defined, begins with the end in mind, and gives more careful consideration to obtaining current and relevant data for both the formative and summative evaluations. Conducted while an intervention is ongoing, formative evaluation provides the feedback necessary to guide and improve the intervention. When the intervention has stabilized, summative evaluation serves to measure the overall value of the intervention (Rodriguez-Campos, 2005). Summative evaluation answers questions such as: Were the anticipated results achieved? Were the outcomes worth the cost and effort to achieve and sustain the results? Leading indicators, described earlier, are critical to the formative evaluation whereas lagging indicators are more useful for the summative evaluation.

Evaluation Models—No One Size Fits All

Various methods and models exist for evaluation, and each varies somewhat in complexity and structure. However, not every method fits every institution's needs. The experience and preferences of those involved in the design and evaluation process may lead some institutions to use one method or model whereas others may prefer to use a different, but similarly effective method. As such, we briefly describe three models and provide references for further exploration.

Prominent among evaluation models is the logic model. The logic model can serve as a planning tool for an intervention strategy, helps organize the planning and the evaluation functions, and can be useful to the institution in identifying and collecting data needed for monitoring and evaluation (W.K. Kellogg Foundation, 2006). Logic models typically include four primary sections: inputs, activities, outputs, and outcomes. Data are arranged from left to right in a table often displayed on a single page with accompanying detail on separate pages. A logic model may show the interaction of these sections as a visual flowchart, which captures the essence of the intervention. In other cases, the model simply lists items under each section. The W. K. Kellogg Foundation (2006) *Logic Model Development Guide* does an excellent job of detailing how to develop logic models and provides templates, checklists, and examples. Another useful resource is Rincones-Gomez (2009) who explains and provides examples of logic models.

Another model, improvement science, is an integral component of the Carnegie Foundation's highly successful Community Colleges Pathways developmental math initiative. The improvement science model asks three deceptively simple questions to guide the development of *both* the intervention and its evaluation (Bryk et al., 2015, p. 114). The questions include: (1) "What specifically are we trying to accomplish? (2) What change might we introduce and why? (3) How will we know that a change is actually an improvement?" Langley et al. (2009, p. 5) note, "These three questions are combined with the Plan-Do-Study-Act (PDSA) Cycle to form the basis of the model."

The use of the PDSA Cycle builds in formative evaluation, ensuring that evaluation is an ongoing process and not a one-time event or action. A strong feature of the work in adopting an intervention under the guidance of the Carnegie Foundation's networked improvement communities' (NICs) approach is consistent use of the PDSA cycle within the classroom throughout the term. Conditions in one institution differ from others, so the formative evaluation (which is discussed in more detail later) using a PDSA approach is essential (Bryk et al., 2015).

A third model for evaluation is Friedman's Results Accountability Method that "starts with ends and works backward, step by step, to means" (Friedman, 2005, p. 12). The method combines intervention design with the evaluation design. The model begins with an understanding of the

NEW DIRECTIONS FOR COMMUNITY COLLEGES • DOI: 10.1002/cc

conditions the college wants and then identifies indicators, (i.e., how to measure those conditions) baseline outcome(s), and what success looks like if the college performs better than the baseline. The method also identifies strategies and performance measures at this stage. Performance measures in the Results Accountability Method are derived from three primary questions that address both the intervention and its evaluation: (a) How much did we do, (b) How well did we do it, and (c) Is anyone better off?

Designing the Evaluation

It is worth repeating that it is inefficient and sometimes counterproductive to separate evaluation from the intervention; practitioners implementing the intervention need formative information to be able to make adjustments and improvements throughout implementation. We advise that staff and faculty who are directly involved with the intervention be included as part of the evaluation design team. Moreover, the method of data collection should be as clear and simple as possible. Data that have already collected by the institution should be used if and when appropriate. When designing the intervention and its evaluation, Bryk et al. (2015) recommend:

> Improvement requires measures that (a) operationalize a working theory of improvement; (b) are specific to the work processes that are the object of change; (c) have formative value signaling subsequent action useful to consider; (d) are framed in a language that is meaningful to those engaged in the work; (e) produce data accessible in a timely manner; and (f) are embedded in social routines that secure the trust and openness necessary to sustain meaningful change efforts. (p. 101)

Although the evaluation and intervention plans may be interwoven, it is important to ensure that the summative evaluation is conducted independent from the intervention. More specifically, we strongly advise that someone with little or no direct stake in the outcome lead the summative evaluation. Becoming too engaged in or invested in the intervention may compromise the integrity of the summative evaluation. For some projects, particularly those supported by external grant funding, an independent evaluator is essential (i.e., someone outside the institution or at least from outside the unit who is implementing the intervention).

Formative evaluation is a different story. Formative evaluation should occur with greater frequency—perhaps as often as weekly—so as to allow for adjustments in the intervention in a timely way. It is probably best, and in some cases essential, to have those involved in the intervention responsible for collecting and analyzing data for the formative evaluation, as they are in a position to make adjustments to the intervention as needed. However, it is also good practice to keep track of and report the results and changes made to a person or group independent of the work.

New Directions for Community Colleges • DOI: 10.1002/cc

Many Achieving the Dream colleges create data teams composed of faculty and staff members who are comfortable with data-informed decision making, including one or more members with statistical analysis capabilities. This team provides assistance to the institutional research or institutional effectiveness office in a variety of ways including assisting intervention teams with the evaluation design. The team or selected members can provide an independent perspective on interpreting the evaluation data and provide feedback to the intervention team.

Steps in Creating an Evaluation Model

We have presented three evaluation models from the literature. Regardless of the method an institution uses, there are essential steps or components for developing and evaluating an intervention. This model supports most evaluation methods. The first step is for the intervention team to identify a theory of change that includes outlining the situation or problem to be to be resolved. It can be useful to develop a clear picture of the future reality to be achieved. For instance, a college may seek to increase fall-to-fall retention. Results that are desired from the intervention should be identified in terms of observable and measurable outcomes (e.g., increase retention by 5 percentage points within 3 years). The team should work together to develop a clear description of *what* has to change to move from the current to the future reality. The team should then determine *how* to bring about the change by identifying one or more strategies or practices that are expected to generate the change and achieve the desired outcomes. An example of practices that may positively influence retention is mandatory advising for new students combined with the use of an early alert system. Large-scale initiatives may use systems improvement maps and driver diagrams in order to determine the changes needed. Excellent examples of improvement maps and driver diagrams can be found in Bryk et al. (2015). It is important to identify the basic premises the strategies are based on (i.e., research findings and theoretical grounding) and why the college expects the strategies to be effective.

Next, the team should work together to design the implementation plan for the new mandatory advising and early alert initiative. For the purposes of this chapter we emphasize the evaluation aspects of the work. At this point, the team must make a decision whether to use an experimental design with random assignment and a control group or a quasiexperimental design using a comparison group. Within this, the team should identify and prioritize specific performance metrics based on the work done in step 1. Narrowing them to the right balance or combination of what is essential and available is vitally important. Qualitative and quantitative data should be collected and available *from the start of the implementation of the intervention* to support the formative evaluation. It is possible that as the implementation proceeds, some formative data will not be as helpful as originally thought and new formative data may need to be collected. As described later, metrics should include both quantitative and qualitative elements and broadly divide into outputs and outcomes.

The team must also develop evaluation questions and identify how the qualitative and quantitative performance metrics will be used to answer each of the questions. The team should consider whether it would need additional metrics to fully answer the questions. According to Friedman (2005), evaluation questions may include (a) How much did we do? (b) How well did we do it? (c) Regarding effort: How hard did we try and what was our quality of effort? (d) Regarding effect: What change did we produce? What modifications are necessary? Is it time to scale the intervention?

The final step is to develop an evaluation plan in tabular (or another visual) form. The team should list the evaluation questions on the left side and then in succeeding columns and rows specify the following information:

1. The data and information necessary to answer the evaluation questions and to support formative evaluation
2. Sources and procedures for collecting the data and information
3. Analysis methods
4. Responsibilities for carrying out the formative and summative evaluations
5. Due dates (i.e., how frequently the formative evaluation will occur and when the summative evaluation will take place)

At the bottom of the form specify the comparison group(s), that is, the group(s) with which the students in the intervention will be compared to understand whether change has occurred.

Outputs and Outcomes

Both outputs and outcomes mentioned in these steps are essential metrics for an evaluation. Outputs are leading indicators that the intervention will have some effect. The targeted level of activity or reach to be achieved for the intervention to work properly should be specified so the evaluation plan can examine target to actual performance for outputs. Outputs are units of service (Friedman, 2005) such as activity counts (e.g., number of participants or instructors trained) and can provide guidance in answering the question "How much did we do?" Outputs may also be measures of reach, such as 30% of advisors were trained or 40% of math students used the math lab, and can help answer the question, "How well did we do it?"

Similar to the causal chain presented by Brinkerhoff (2006), performance metrics can be thought of as a causal chain; outputs lead to awareness, satisfaction, knowledge and/or skill development, which in turn lead to observable and measurable change in behavior that influences student success outcomes/impacts. Measures of awareness, satisfaction, knowledge and skills development, and observable and measurable behaviors (e.g., class attendance, attending tutoring, seeing an advisor, and grades) can be very useful for the team's formative evaluation. Ongoing monitoring of activities and behaviors should be used to trigger immediate corrective action during implementation.

In terms of summative evaluation, outcomes/impacts may include measures such as course completion, successful achievement of learning objectives, semester or year retention, degree completion, or gainful employment. Outcomes/impacts can be thought of as a second causal chain where short-term outcomes lead or influence longer term outcomes (referred to as impacts). For instance, achieving learning objectives may lead to a short-term outcome (e.g., course success), which may lead to a longer term outcome such as retention, which in turn influences completion of a certificate or degree, which may lead to gainful employment. Outcomes or impacts such as being a better citizen or having a well-rounded education could also be considered although these may be harder to measure. It is important to note that not every intervention will or should be evaluated on all of the outcomes listed here. Rather, some interventions will be expected to affect only part of the causal chain.

Analysis Methods

Descriptive statistics are the first step in analyzing quantitative data collected for an evaluation. Statistics such as percentages and means describe and compare the characteristics, behaviors, and/or outcomes of the participants (both the students receiving the intervention and the control/comparison group). In many cases, descriptive statistics suffice for evaluating an intervention. Inferential statistics (e.g., t-test and ANOVA) can be used to assess whether differences between groups are practically or statistically significant and were unlikely to occur by chance. More advanced techniques such as regression may also be useful in cases where students participated in multiple interventions or to control for other variables related to the outcome. Qualitative data can be extremely valuable in providing a rich description of the students' perceptions and behaviors related to the intervention. Analysis of qualitative data may involve identifying patterns or themes in the data to answer "how" or "why" questions.

We suggest including someone with a solid statistical background (e.g., research analyst or faculty member) as part of the team or in an advisory role. This person will be able to suggest types of data that need to be collected to answer the evaluation questions and provide formative feedback. An analyst will also be able to suggest when further, more complex statistical analyses are needed. We caution, however, to always keep the analysis methods as simple as possible to avoid costly and complex evaluations in relation to the scope and magnitude of the intervention. This might be thought of as a trade-off between the "good enough" and the perfect scientific evidence. Realistically, "good enough" may be appropriate for many interventions.

Often-Overlooked Evaluation Topics

Although the impact of the intervention on student success should be the primary consideration in evaluation, return on investment (ROI), sustainability, and scalability are evaluation issues that warrant mention. Return on investment requires consideration of the value of the effort, usually measured in monetary terms, compared with the savings or the actual revenue gain resulting from student retention. No community college has unlimited resources, and if the cost of an intervention greatly outstrips the value of the end results, it may need to be redesigned or reconsidered altogether. There are also other "value" metrics, including the value of positive relations with the community and long-term benefits to students' well-being. In our experience, ROI is, however, an often-overlooked consideration in developing and implementing evaluations. Additional information on return on investments in student success along with an Excel-based calculator can be found at: http://www.jff.org/publications/calculating -cost-return-investments-student-success.

Related to ROI are sustainability and scalability. Grant-funded interventions generally require institutions to develop a plan to continue the actions after the grant funding ends, but even for internally funded interventions, this practice is an important consideration in evaluation. Can the institution continue the quantity and quality of effort over the longer term? If an intervention is reliant on the good will of volunteers, efforts might not be sustainable. On the other hand, if an intervention can be embedded as part of a continuing institutional process or program, it is more likely to be sustained.

Finally, there is scalability. Offering valuable services to a small percentage of the student population is unlikely to "move the needle" in student success metrics. On the other hand, scaling up from a small pilot group to the entire population can be challenging, especially when the demographics of the pilot program are not representative of the larger population. Examples of this are abundant in other fields, notably medicine where the effectiveness of a medication is found to be different for different groups (e.g., females and males). Likewise, the impact(s) of an intervention on a group of students who are motivated enough to volunteer to participate may be very different results when the intervention is expanded to a broader group of students (e.g., issue of selection bias). Moreover, an intervention that is scaled up may not have any overall significant effect on success outcomes. An intervention that fails to demonstrate significant impacts should not necessarily be abandoned, however.

Instead, perform additional analyses to identify whether the intervention was more or less effective for particular subgroups (e.g., first generation and racial/ethnic groups) that may identify the value in a more targeted approach. Additional information on sustainability and scaling of interventions is available in a guide to scaling community college interventions at http://www.publicagenda.org/files/CuttingEdge2.pdf.

Final Thoughts

Evaluation is an essential part of student success efforts and should to be designed at the same time teams design the intervention(s) aiming to improve student success. Evaluations, when well done, can assist community colleges in staying on track of intervention goals/objectives through consistent and frequent formative evaluation and improvement. A well-designed summative evaluation can provide the basis for decisions to continue or scale up interventions by providing data regarding particular elements of the intervention that had the desired impact. The combination of formative and summative evaluations is a series of value judgments based on well-defined, agreed-upon, defensible criteria that can set an institution's interventions on a path toward realization of improved student success outcomes.

Ultimately, we feel that it is important to find and follow a method of evaluation that fits the needs of the college, is not more complex than needed to answer the evaluation questions, and does not present unrealistic data collection or analysis challenges. Moreover, development and follow-through on an evaluation plan with timelines, shared responsibility, and relevant data elements are vitally important.

Notes

1. Interventions or programs designed to improve student success are based on a theory of change, that is, if the institution does X it will result in Y effect. Further detail is provided in the later part of the chapter.
2. In this chapter retention means term-to-term retention and/or year-to-year retention.

References

Berlin, G. (2014). Impact on a large scale: The importance of evidence. New York, NY: MDRC. Retrieved from http://www.mdrc.org/sites/default/files/Impact%20on%20a%20Large%20Scale%20_web.pdf

Brinkerhoff, R. O. (2006). Telling training's story: Evaluation made simple, credible, and effective. San Francisco, CA: Berrett-Koehler.

Bryk, A. S., Gomez, L. M., Grunow, A., & LeMahieu, P. G. (2015). Learning to improve: How America's schools can get better at getting better. Cambridge, MA. Harvard Education Press.

Friedman, M. (2005). Trying hard is not good enough. Victoria, BC, Canada: Trafford Press.

Gendron, S. A., & Traub, S. (2015). *Leading and lagging indicators to inform systemwide change.* Rexford, NY: International Center for Leadership Education. Retrieved from http://leadered.com/pdf/ICLELeadingLaggingIndicatorsSB.pdf

Hess, F. M., & Little, B. (2015). *Moneyball for education: Using data, evidence, and evaluation to improve federal education policy.* Washington, DC: American Enterprise Institute. Retrieved from https://www.aei.org/wp-content/uploads/2015/03/Moneyball-for-education.pdf

Langley, G. J., Moen, R. D., Nolan, K. M., Nolan, T. W., Norman, C. L., & Provost, L. P. (2009). *The improvement guide: A practical approach to enhancing organizational performance.* San Francisco, CA: Jossey-Bass.

Rincones-Gomez, R. J. (2009). *Evaluating student success interventions: Principles and practices of student success.* Silver Spring, MD: Achieving the Dream. Retrieved from http://www.achievingthedream.org/resource/177/evaluating-student-success-interventions-principles-and-practices-of-student-success

Rodriguez-Campos, L. (2005). *Collaborative evaluations: A step-by-step model for the evaluator.* Tamarac, FL: Lumina Press.

W. K. Kellogg Foundation. (2006). *Logic model development guide.* Battle, Creek, MI: Author. Retrieved from https://www.wkkf.org/resource-directory/resource/2006/02/wk-kellogg-foundation-logic-model-development-guide

BRUCE E. MCCOMB *and* JAN W. LYDDON, *PhD, are principals of Organizational Effectiveness Consultants (OEC). They are both Data Coaches with Achieving the Dream.*

NEW DIRECTIONS FOR COMMUNITY COLLEGES • DOI: 10.1002/cc

8

This chapter provides an overview of organizations and other entities focused on assisting community college staff, faculty, and administrators in developing and promoting student success outcomes. We provide a listing of relevant web resources related to programming and conclude with a summary of suggested readings.

Key Resources for Community College Student Success Programming

Vincent D. Carales, Crystal E. Garcia, Naomi Mardock-Uman

The continuously evolving mission of community colleges and the increasingly diverse student population these institutions serve present both opportunities and challenges for practitioners, researchers, and policy makers. In addition, the growing focus on college completion has placed community colleges in the spotlight in terms of increasing positive student outcomes (Lester, 2014). As the number of students who begin their postsecondary experience at community colleges continues to grow, it is crucial for community college personnel to understand the approaches, strategies, and practices that best serve these students and to find ways to increase their educational attainment and success.

This chapter complements information provided throughout this issue by offering key resources and relevant research to assist community college staff, faculty, and administrators in developing, implementing, and evaluating promising and high-impact programs and practices. We provide descriptions of national organizations that promote student success programming and research at community colleges. We also outline resources and readings that address a variety of practices that have potential to foster positive community college student outcomes or that highlight model programs at community colleges around the country.

National Organizations

The following national organizations support success programs at US community colleges.

Achieving the Dream. The Lumina Foundation and seven other partner organizations initiated Achieving the Dream as a means of establishing

NEW DIRECTIONS FOR COMMUNITY COLLEGES, no. 175, Fall 2016 © 2016 Wiley Periodicals, Inc.
Published online in Wiley Online Library (wileyonlinelibrary.com) • DOI: 10.1002/cc.20215

a comprehensive national reform network to strengthen the community college system. The website's resource page is divided into four subareas: a knowledge center including guides, case studies, and reports; information on active and former initiatives; research and publications covering technology solutions that can assist in supporting student success; and interventions employed by member institutions that can be viewed by type, academic discipline, or by college. http://www.achievingthedream.org/

Key Web Resource.   Focus Areas. The Focus Areas tab on the Achieving the Dream website divides 14 focus areas into icons that, when selected, provide a description along with a list of resources and interventions.

American Association of Community Colleges.   The American Association of Community Colleges (AACC) supports and advocates for nearly 1,200 community colleges through a variety of strategic initiatives. Part of the mission of AACC is to provide resources and information to create and facilitate opportunities for peer networking and interaction, leadership, and career development for community college personnel. Practitioners can use AACC's host of reports, white papers, and research briefs to stay current on important trends and issues related to community colleges. http://www.aacc.nche.edu/Pages/default.aspx

Key Web Resources.   Data Points. These data publication archives provide snapshots of timely and important topics related to community colleges including dual enrollment, developmental education, transfer outcomes, student mobility and educational attainment.

Community College Trends and Statistics. This section contains a wide variety of statistical and trend information on community colleges and their students, faculty, and staff including information on enrollment, financial aid, educational attainment, and faculty, staff, and institutional characteristics of community colleges.

Center for Community College Student Engagement.   Best known for its surveys of community college students and faculty, the Center for Community College Student Engagement (CCCSE) in the College of Education at the University of Texas at Austin conducts research and works with community and technical colleges throughout the United States on student engagement and success. CCCSE connects student engagement to student learning, retention, and attainment through initiatives such as *High-Impact Practices, Latino Student Engagement and Transfer*, and *Aspirations to Achievement: Men of Color and Community Colleges*. CCCSE disseminates findings from its initiatives in national reports that are available on its website, which also includes videos from the center's student focus group work and newsletters. http://www.ccsse.org/center/

Key Web Resources.   CCCSE Reports. A Matter of Degrees: Promising Practices for Community College Students (2012), *A Matter of Degrees: Engaging Practices, Engaging Students* (2013), and *A Matter of Degrees: Practices to Pathways* (2014) present the key findings from the High-Impact Practice Initiative.

Community College Institutional Survey (CCIS) Discussion Guide. Intended for use in conjunction with institutional CCIS results, this document presents questions to facilitate campus conversions around high-impact practices (see Waiwaiole, Bohlig, and Massey's chapter in this volume).

Community College Research Center (CCRC).   Housed at Teachers College, Columbia University, CCRC's research and collaborations focus on current areas of concern to community colleges including high school-to-college transition, developmental education and adult basic skills, student services and financial aid, online education and instructional technology, student persistence, completion and transfer, college-to-career and workforce education, and the role of the community college. CCRC also leads two research centers funded by grants from the U.S. Department of Education's Institute of Education Sciences: the Center for the Analysis of Postsecondary Readiness (CAPR) and the Center for Analysis of Postsecondary Education and Employment (CAPSEE). The CCRC web resources are divided into three different sections for administrators and faculty, institutional researchers, and policy makers. http://ccrc.tc.columbia.edu

Key Web Resource.   Selected Resources. These resource publications and practitioner packets provide research-based evidence in key student success topic areas including assessment and placement, advising, guided pathways, and the student experience.

Council for the Study of Community Colleges (CSCC).   CSCC is a project of the Center for the Study of Community Colleges and an affiliate of the American Association of Community Colleges. The council is composed of community college scholars and practitioners engaged in developing community college scholarship. The council serves to disseminate research related to community colleges and develop community college professionals. http://www.cscconline.org

Key Web Resource.   Research and Reports Blog. CSCC's reports blog offers a searchable database of research projects and articles related to community colleges. An abstract and citation is provided for each resource.

National Academic Advising Association (NACADA).   NACADA is a global community of academic advisors that promotes and supports high-quality academic advising in institutions of higher education to enhance student development. The association provides academic advisors with a variety of reference materials, including the Clearinghouse of Academic Advising Resources, the quarterly online publication *Academic Advising Today*, and the biannual, refereed *NACADA Journal*. http://www.nacada.ksu.edu/

Key Web Resource.   Research Listserv. The NACADA Research Committee sponsors a research discussion listserv to stimulate communication among those researching advising topics.

National Center for Developmental Education.   The National Center for Developmental Education (NCDE) in the Reich College of Education at Appalachian State University conducts research, provides professional development and consultation for practitioners and institutions, and houses a collection of resources related to the field of developmental education and learning assistance. NCDE publishes the *Journal of Developmental Education* and *Research in Developmental Education* as well as books and reports, some of which are available via the center's website. http://ncde.appstate.edu/

Key Web Resource.   Reports and Research. NCDE's website offers full-text (PDF) access to selected articles from the center's two academic journals and to reports from external sources. Topics include assessment and placement, developmental education program evaluation, and promising practices in the field.

National Resource Center for The First-Year Experience and Students in Transition.   The National Resource Center for The First-Year Experience and Students in Transition works to bolster student learning and support transitions throughout the higher education pipeline by engaging in conversations regarding institutional practices and disseminating research and publications to the greater higher education community. The center offers conferences, institutes, workshops, and online courses in diverse areas related to the first-year experience and students in transition and conducts national research on issues relevant to college student success—including high-impact practices. The center also conducts a series of annual surveys and includes links to the surveys and executive summaries on the organization's website. http://www.sc.edu/fye/

Key Web Resource.   The Toolbox. The Toolbox is a free online professional development newsletter published six times a year. It offers instructors strategies and resources to enrich the educational environment.

National Resource Center for Learning Communities.   The Washington Center at Evergreen State College supports the establishment of effective learning communities in community colleges and 4-year institutions in Washington and across the United States. The organization serves institutions and programs through a number of initiatives including helping campus teams establish effective learning community programs, providing professional development opportunities aimed at enhancing teaching effectiveness, and connecting campuses and communities through targeted projects. The center's site offers information and readings for professional development as well as suggestions and resources for various forms of assessment including assessment of integrative learning, classrooms, programs, and students' learning experiences. http://www.evergreen.edu/washingtoncenter/

Key Web Resource.   Resources Page. The resources page offers links to a number of publications categorized by various areas and issues faced by institutions of higher education.

Suggested Readings

This chapter was designed to connect readers with key resources that shed light on ways in which promising community college institutional practices

Table 8.1   Suggested Readings

Citation	Practices Addressed	Description
Brownell, J. E., & Swaner, L. E. (2009). High-impact practices: Applying the learning outcomes literature to the development of successful campus programs. *Peer Review*, *11*(2), 26–30.	First-year seminars, learning communities, service learning, undergraduate research	Provides a brief literature review and critique of the outcomes associated with high-impact practices. Includes suggestions on how campuses can implement these practices in their own program design.
Cho, S., & Karp, M. M. (2013). Student success courses in the community college: Early enrollment and educational outcomes. *Community College Review*, *41*(1), 86–103.	Student success courses	Examines the association between enrollment in a student success course and short-term educational outcomes and student persistence.
Crisp, G., & Taggart, A. (2013). Community college student success programs: A synthesis, critique, and research agenda. *Community College Journal of Research and Practice*, *37*(2), 114–130.	Learning communities, student success courses, supplemental instruction	Focuses on the assessment and impact of student success programs at community colleges. Includes recommendations for further research related to program effectiveness and intervention efforts.
Jaggars, S. S., Hodara, M., Cho, S., & Xu, D. (2015). Three accelerated developmental education programs: Features, student outcomes, and implications. *Community College Review*, *43*(1), 3–26.	Accelerated developmental education courses	Presents findings on the impact and program assessment of accelerated developmental education programs at three community colleges. Also offers three considerations for future program implementation.
Karp, M. M. (2011). Toward a new understanding of non-academic student support: Four mechanisms encouraging positive student outcomes in the community college (CCRC Working Paper No. 28). New York, NY: Columbia University, Teachers College, Community College Research Center.	Learning communities, student success courses, enhanced/intrusive advising	Analyzes empirical evidence along with the combination of persistence theory and program evaluation literature and demonstrates how practitioners can improve nonacademic support efforts in helping students succeed. Four important approaches are highlighted.

(Continued)

NEW DIRECTIONS FOR COMMUNITY COLLEGES • DOI: 10.1002/cc

Table 8.1   Continued

Citation	Practices Addressed	Description
Karp, M. M., Bickerstaff, S. E., Rucks-Ahidiana, Z., Bork, R. J. H., Barragan, M., & Edgecombe, N. D. (2012). *College 101 courses for applied learning and student success* (CCRC Working Paper No. 49). New York, NY: Columbia University, Teachers College, Community College Research Center.	First-year experience, orientation, student success courses	Qualitatively examines the nature and implementation of College 101 courses (also identified by other names such as a student success course) using a theory of action to identify practices that lead to positive student outcomes.
Pike, G. R., Kuh, G. D., & McCormick, A. C. (2011). An investigation of the contingent relationships between learning community participation and student engagement. *Research in Higher Education, 52*(3), 300–322.	Learning communities	Uses data from the National Survey of Student Engagement (NSSE) to examine the relationship between participation in learning communities and six measures of student engagement (academic effort, integrative and higher-order thinking, diversity experiences, active and collaborative learning, student–faculty interaction, and supportive campus environment).
Price, D. V., & Tovar, E. (2014). Student engagement and institutional graduation rates: Identifying high-impact educational practices for community colleges. *Community College Journal of Research and Practice, 38*(9), 766–782.	Learning communities, supplemental instruction, tutoring	Uses data from the Community College Survey of Student Engagement (CCSSE) and the Integrated Postsecondary Education Data System (IPEDS) to examine college completion rates in relation to CCSSE's student engagement benchmarks (active and collaborative learning, student effort, academic challenge, student-faculty interaction, and support for learners). Also offers classroom and institutional implications for practice.

(Continued)

Table 8.1   Continued

Citation	Practices Addressed	Description
Roksa, J., Jenkins, D., Jaggars, S. S., Zeidenberg, M., & Cho, S. W. (2009). *Strategies for promoting gatekeeper course success among students needing remediation: Research report for the Virginia Community College System*. New York, NY: Columbia University, Teachers College, Community College Research Center.	Assessment and placement, accelerated or fast-track developmental education	Reports the findings of a quantitative study conducted by the Community College Research Center on the policies and practices of developmental instruction in the Virginia Community College System. Includes recommendations for promoting the success of students in gatekeeper courses.
Saxon, D. P., & Morante, E. A. (2014). Effective student assessment and placement: Challenges and recommendations. *Journal of Developmental Education*, 37(3), 24–29.	Assessment and placement, academic goal setting and planning, registration before classes begin	Addresses recent criticisms in the research literature of the use of assessment and placement measures in community colleges and describes challenges institutions face in implementing them effectively. The author recommends a comprehensive system including high-quality advising and developmental education programs for at-risk students.
Visher, M. G., Weiss, M. J., Weissman, E., Rudd, T., & Wathington, H. D. (2012). *The effects of learning communities for students in developmental education: A synthesis of findings from six community colleges*. New York: Columbia University, Teachers College, National Center for Postsecondary Research.	Learning communities	Presents an analysis of community college learning communities implemented for the purpose of this study by the National Center for Postsecondary Research. Includes implications for practitioners and policy makers.
Weiss, M. J., Mayer, A., Cullinan, D., Ratledge, A., Sommo, C., & Diamond, J. (2014). *A random assignment evaluation of learning communities at Kingsborough Community College: Seven years later.* New York: MDRC.	Learning communities	Presents the results of a long-term follow-up study of a community college learning community, including the program's impact on students' academic progress, degree completion, and economic outcomes.

(Continued)

Table 8.1   Continued

Citation	Practices Addressed	Description
Zaritsky, J. S., & Toce, A. (2006). Supplemental instruction at a community college: The four pillars. In M. E. Stone & G. Jacobs (Eds.), *New Directions for Teaching and Learning: No. 106. Supplemental instruction: New visions for empowering student learning* (pp. 23–31). San Francisco, CA: Jossey-Bass.	Supplemental instruction	Describes a voluntary supplemental instruction (SI) program at one community college where advanced students are employed as instructional leaders. Includes an analysis of the impact of SI session attendance on student grades.

can be implemented and sustained. In addition to the organizations and key web resources identified in this chapter, we offer the following suggested readings in Table 8.1 that focus on a variety of these initiatives and related practices.

Reference

Lester, J. (2014). The completion agenda: The unintended consequences for equity in community colleges. In M. B. Paulsen (Ed.), *Higher education: Handbook of theory and research* (Vol. 29, pp. 423–466). Dordrecht, the Netherlands: Springer.

VINCENT D. CARALES *is a doctoral fellow at the University of Texas at San Antonio.*

CRYSTAL E. GARCIA *is a doctoral candidate at the University of Nebraska–Lincoln.*

NAOMI MARDOCK-UMAN *is a doctoral student at the University of Nebraska–Lincoln.*

NEW DIRECTIONS FOR COMMUNITY COLLEGES • DOI: 10.1002/cc

9

The final chapter of the issue provides a synthesis of the first eight chapters, offers conclusions and recommendations, and considers future directions regarding practices and programs with promise for high impact at community colleges around the country.

Promising Practices and Programs: Current Efforts and Future Directions

Gloria Crisp

Community colleges and their students have received growing attention from policy makers, foundations, and scholars since the 1990s and are currently at the forefront of national higher education reform efforts (Harbour, 2015). The American Association of Community Colleges (AACC, 2012) has recommended that community colleges develop "coherent, structured pathways to certificate and degree completion" that incorporate "high-impact, evidence-based educational practices" (p. 26). Community colleges continue to be willing to experiment with various practices and programs in search of the magic potion that will substantively improve success outcomes (Levin, Cox, Cerven, & Haberler, 2010). However, no single practice or program is a panacea and a substantial amount of work remains for innovative practices and programs to be effectively incorporated into student pathways at community colleges throughout the country. In this final chapter, I provide a synthesis of key ideas/themes to detail ways the individual chapters and volume as a whole contribute to existing knowledge. I then offer observations and recommendations that I believe to be central to moving research forward toward supporting community colleges in meeting national completion goals.

Key Ideas/Themes

Collectively, the work of my colleagues in this volume highlights the importance of implementing and evaluating what are increasingly referred to as "high-impact" or "promising" practices and programs as a means to help support the nation's completion goals. In Chapter 5, Young and Keup offer a compelling argument for why first-year seminars are one of the most

NEW DIRECTIONS FOR COMMUNITY COLLEGES, no. 175, Fall 2016 © 2016 Wiley Periodicals, Inc.
Published online in Wiley Online Library (wileyonlinelibrary.com) • DOI: 10.1002/cc.20216

promising practices for supporting students' transitions to college and how community colleges are currently structuring them in relation to other promising practices. The value of first-year seminars/experiences is reinforced in Chapter 6 by Acevedo-Gil and Zerquera who provide qualitative evidence that various practices/programs can be designed within a first-year experience (FYE) and support students' transitions to college.

The volume as a whole also provides needed information about what promising practices and programs look like in a community college context. In Chapter 4, Waiwaiole and Bohlig describe outcomes of the Center for Community College Student Engagement's High-Impact Practice (HIP) Institutes. This description adds to our understanding regarding the important work that is being done across community college campuses. Moreover, the case study examples provided in Chapter 4 shed light on the processes community colleges are using to enhance and redesign programs and practices to enrich students' experiences. Jointly, but particularly in Chapter 6, the chapters also make a strong argument for the worth of students' voices in understanding how and why programs and practices can be effective in supporting students' pathways to degree completion.

The volume brings attention to the absence of clear, consistent terminology and frameworks to understand if and how programs and practices may be meaningfully different and/or conceptually similar. Namely, Chapter 1 provides an overview of definitions of prevalent promising practices and programs. Importantly, the issue also offers alternative ways to conceptualize various practices and programs, which has the potential to guide practitioners in redesigning, combining, and/or enhancing practices. For instance, Chapter 4 illustrates ways community colleges are using different names to describe programs with the same content and note considerable overlap in the curricular and programmatic elements across different programs and practices. Conceptually, Young and Keup and Acevedo-Gil and Zerquera offer first-year experience programs as a place to connect students to other promising practices and programs. Likewise, Chapters 5 and 6 demonstrate how other programs/practices may be effectively integrated within a first-year experience (e.g., learning communities and advising). Moreover, extending his recent work, Hatch offers Cultural Historical Activity Theory (CHAT) in Chapter 2 as a means of conceptualizing programs as instances of a more general type of program and an explanation of why certain programs resemble one another to configure what he terms a structured group socialization experience.

In other ways, however, the volume adds clarity regarding the ways in which programs and practices can be meaningfully distinguished from each other beginning in Chapter 1 with a visual map of program features and relationships. Young and Keup (Chapter 5) note that the timing can differentiate first-year seminars, because they are, by definition, offered in the first year of college. Additionally, in Chapter 3, Karp distinguishes practices/programs by the type(s) of support offered, identifying four key mechanisms or "things that happen" in the context of programs and practices: (a) creating social relationships, (b) clarifying aspirations and enhancing commitment, (c) developing college know-how, and (d) making college life feasible. Similarly, findings from Chapter 6 by Acevedo-Gil and Zerquera suggest that programs may be distinguished by the involvement of various individuals including advisors and faculty who support students. Importantly, the authors identify specific types of support provided to students by what might be called mentors (Crisp, 2009) or institutional agents (Stanton-Salazar, 2011) as part of a first-year seminar.

Finally, the chapters in this volume contribute practical guidance to community colleges in designing and evaluating promising practices and programs. In Chapter 3, Karp offers practical uses of her framework of nonacademic support, encouraging colleges to design and implement practices and programs that are holistic and multifaceted. Hatch (Chapter 2) explains how CHAT can be used by community college personnel in considering collectively the goals, available curricular tools, and social contexts of all participants when designing, evaluating, and improving programs. Chapter 7, written by Achieving the Dream (AtD) coaches McComb and Lyddon, contributes extensive field-based experiences in providing guidance to colleges in determining whether efforts are promising or high impact and offers practical information and advice for evaluating interventions on community college campuses. Chapter 8 by Carales, Garcia, and Mardock Uman is dedicated entirely to presenting key resources and research to community colleges in program design, implementation, and evaluation.

Observations and Recommendations

Next, I offer some observations and recommendations for moving forward the important work of identifying high-impact programs and practices. My thoughts are grounded by what I perceive as the unavoidable and mounting tension between implementing specific programs and practices tailored to the needs of particular groups of students and redesigning the entire student experience around effective practices and policies for broader impacts. Harbour (2015) argues that colleges should create their own community-based movements and programs dedicated to developing locally based solutions. In many, if not all cases, this requires designing a diversity of "boutique" services and programs designed to meet the specific needs of students at individual colleges (Mellow & Heelan, 2008). Although desirable, boutique programs are generally not economical and exclude the majority of students on campus. Incremental improvements to local programs and services are unlikely to substantially contribute to meeting broader completion goals (Jenkins, 2015). In my experiences with community colleges, I've increasingly witnessed and felt colleges being pressured to scale up, combine, and restructure promising practices and programs to reach broader groups of students. It is notable that these persuasions appear to be both externally and internally driven. In addition to AACC's (2012) recommendations for colleges to implement and scale up high-impact practices, the Center for Community College Student Engagement report (CCCSE, 2014) has advised that colleges build practices into every student's educational experience. At the same time, community college faculty and staff are increasingly expected by the campus/district administration to scale up promising practices, which often requires obtaining external funding and/or reallocating resources from current services.

The challenge of identifying practices and programs that are not only effective but also generalizable to other populations and campuses is considerable (Haberler & Levin, 2014). A review of existing evidence identifies several notable limitations currently impeding practitioners' ability to develop and implement effective, scalable practices (see Crisp & Taggart, 2013). It should be noted that many of these limitations stem from a research base that has been largely focused on understanding program outcomes at single institutions rather than broad impacts research that attempts to draw generalizations and scale up work (Bers & Younger, 2014). Researchers have largely focused efforts on a small set of programs that include orientation, first-year experiences, success courses, learning communities, and accelerated developmental education.

A review of existing evidence suggests first-year experiences may be effective in promoting retention/persistence among community college students (Crisp & Taggart, 2013). Similarly, recent findings indicate that participation in learning communities may be positively related to a range of community college outcomes including retention, course completion, grades, integration, and graduation rates (e.g., Scrivener & Coghlan, 2011). Most recently, one of the few and the largest independent randomized trials in this area conducted by Weiss, Visher, Weissman, & Wathington (2015) found that the overall average effects (in this case, on credits earned) of learning communities for students enrolled in developmental education at six colleges tended to be positive, although modest. Likewise, there is non-experimental evidence to suggest a positive relationship between enrollment in a student success course and short-term outcomes including persistence and credit attainment (Cho & Karp, 2013). The quality and amount of empirical evidence are uneven across programs and practices, however. Although there is mounting evidence supporting the value of structured group learning experiences, studies/evaluations have not always revealed a positive relationship between such efforts and community college students' experiences and outcomes (e.g., Richburg-Hayes, Visher, & Bloom, 2008). In fact, it may not be uncommon for students to have negative experiences with programs and practices (Talburt & Boyles, 2005).

A substantial amount of research remains to be done to guide practitioners in implementing practices and programs that are in fact high impact and can meaningfully improve completion rates at community colleges

(Scrivener & Coghlan, 2011). In particular, research is needed to better understand the programmatic features that contribute the most to student outcomes (Hatch, 2012; Schnee, 2014). Many practices reflect "evidence-based hypotheses" regarding how community colleges can support students' pathways to completion rather than proven solutions (Bailey & Smith Jaggars, 2015). There is limited evidence that effective practices should incorporate principles of active and collaborative learning (Price & Tovar, 2014). Still, most of what is known regarding students' experiences with practices and programs is derived from surveys that do not allow room for students' voices or what their experiences mean to them in the broader context of their goals and educational pathway (Finley & McNair, 2013). Following the recommendation of Schnee (2014), I suggest researchers give attention to capturing students' perceptions, experiences, and voices regarding practices and programs. It is expected that qualitative data will help to identify specific programmatic components that can be examined within larger scale program evaluations. If/when they are shown to be effective, identified components can be used in redesign and enhancing promising practices.

In Chapter 5, Acevedo-Gil and Zerquera note that with practices and programs, the whole is greater than the sum of its parts. Findings demonstrate a variety of practices that individually may be related to success outcomes. However, relatively little is known about the combined and cumulative impacts of multiple practices/programs. There is evidence that fusing programs and services may lead to greater impacts on success when compared to individual practices or programs (e.g., Scrivener, Weiss, Sommo, & Fresques, 2012). Given the fiscal constraints facing community colleges, it is rarely, if ever, feasible (or likely necessary) to make all promising practices and programs available to every community college student. Moving forward, I recommend that attention be given to scholarship that examines if and how program components can be most efficiently and effectively combined to foster success.

As shown in Chapter 1, there is a great deal of overlap and inconsistency in the terms used to describe and distinguish between practices and programs (also see work by Hatch & Bohlig, 2015). Collectively, these variations serve to impede the development, implementation, evaluation, and comparison of efforts (Crisp & Taggart, 2013). In order to make sense of and provide clarity to how practices and programs are defined and used, Hatch (2012) argues that practices be considered more "structurally, systematically, and collectively" (p. 909), identifying programs by what goes into them rather than by their name. At the same time, experience has taught me the necessity of having a commonly understood language when engaging in programmatic work. Regardless of the term(s) or language that is used, it is important for practitioners to have *clarity* and *consensus* when designing practices and programs (see key features in Chapter 1). Likewise,

I suggest that researchers be mindful of including descriptive operational definitions for all programs being studied when presenting and publishing their work.

"Program practices derive more from people than they do from policies, and promising practices derive especially from the adaptability of those involved with the program, including faculty members, staff members, and administrators" (Levin et al., 2010, p. 54). Acevedo-Gil and Zerquera's work in this volume suggests that key individuals including advisors, faculty, and peers play a central role in shaping students' experiences with practices and programs. These findings suggest that various forms of mentoring support (Crisp, 2009) should be given consideration and examination as a promising practice/program. Finally, drawing from CHAT and other sociological and ecological theories, I recommend attention be provided to developing a deeper theoretical and empirical understanding how the college environment/context and institutional conditions are serving to promote or inhibit students' experiences and subsequent programmatic outcomes.

Final Thought

Progress toward meeting national completion goals will require continued, coordinated, and focused participation and commitment from community college administrators, faculty and staff, community college scholars, and researchers representing centers and federally funded projects. More than this, meaningful progress will require stakeholders to identify spaces in which to purposefully come together to share ideas and collaborate in designing, implementing, and evaluating promising practices and programs. The present volume of New Directions for Community Colleges is an example of how community college practice and scholarship can be strengthened by bringing the ideas and perspectives of various groups together. I am hopeful that our issue will serve as a means of continuing conversations as well as beginning/developing collaborations focused toward community college student success.

References

American Association of Community Colleges. (2012). Reclaiming the American Dream: A report from the 21st-Century Commission on the Future of Community Colleges. Washington, DC: Author. Retrieved from http://www.aacc.nche.edu/21stCenturyReport

Bailey, T. R., & Smith Jaggars, S. (2015). Redesigning America's community colleges: A clearer path to student success. Cambridge, MA: Harvard University Press.

Bers, T., & Younger, D. (2014). The first-year experience in community colleges. In R. D. Padgett (Ed.), New Directions for Institutional Research: No. 160. Emerging research and practices on first-year students (pp. 77–93). San Francisco, CA: Jossey-Bass.

Center for Community College Student Engagement. (2014). A matter of degrees: Practices to pathways (High-impact practices for community college student success). Austin, TX: The University of Texas at Austin, Program in Higher Education Leadership.

Cho, S-W., & Karp, M. M. (2013). Student success courses in the community college: Early enrollment and educational outcomes. *Community College Review*, *41*(1), 86–103.

Crisp, G. (2009). Conceptualization and initial validation of the College Student Mentoring Scale (CSMS). *Journal of College Student Development*, *50*(2), 177–194. doi:10.1353/csd.0.0061

Crisp, G., & Taggart, A. (2013). Community college student success programs: A synthesis, critique, and research agenda. *Community College Journal of Research and Practice*, *37*(2), 114–130.

Finley, A., & McNair, T. (2013). *Assessing underserved students' engagement in high-impact practices*. Washington, DC: Association of American Colleges & Universities. Retrieved from http://www.aacu.org/sites/default/files/files/assessinghips/AssessingHIPS_TGGrantReport.pdf

Haberler, Z., & Levin, J. S. (2014). The four Cs of promising practices in community colleges. *Community College Journal of Research and Practice*, *38*(5), 403–416. doi:10.1080/10668926.2012.748381

Harbour, C. P. (2015). *John Dewey and the future of community college education*. London: Bloomsbury Academic.

Hatch, D. K. (2012). Unpacking the black box of student engagement: The need for programmatic investigation of high-impact practices. *Community College Journal of Research and Practice*. *36*(11), 903–915. doi:10.1080/10668926.2012.690319

Hatch, D. K., & Bohlig, E. M. (2015). The scope and design of structured group learning experiences at community colleges. *Community College Journal of Research and Practice*, *39*(9), 819–838. doi:10.1080/10668926.2014.911128

Jenkins, D. (2015). Community College Research Center: Collaborative research to improve student success. *Community College Journal of Research and Practice*, *39*(10), 933–937, doi:10.1080/10668926.2015.1033780

Levin, J. S., Cox, E. M., Cerven, C., & Haberler, Z. (2010). The recipe for promising practices in community colleges. *Community College Review*, *38*(1), 31–58.

Mellow, G. O., & Heelan, C. (2008). *Minding the dream: The process and practice of the American community college*. Lanham, MD: Rowman & Littlefield.

Price, D. V., & Tovar, E. (2014). Student engagement and institutional graduation rates: Identifying high-impact educational practices for community colleges. *Community College Journal of Research and Practice*, *38*(9), 766–782. doi:10.1080/10668926.2012.719481

Richburg-Hayes, L., Visher, M. G., & Bloom, D. (2008). Do learning communities affect academic outcomes? Evidence from an experiment in a community college. *Journal of Research on Educational Effectiveness*, *1*(1), 33–65.

Schnee, E. (2014). "A foundation for something bigger": Community college students' experience of remediation in the context of a learning community. *Community College Review*, *42*(3), 242–261.

Scrivener, S., & Coghlan, E. (2011). *Opening doors to student success: A synthesis of findings from an evaluation at six community colleges*. New York, NY: MDRC.

Scrivener, S., Weiss, M., Sommo, C., & Fresques, H. (2012). *What can a multifaceted program do for community college students? Early results from an evaluation of accelerated study in associate programs (ASAP) for developmental education students*. New York, NY: MDRC.

Stanton-Salazar, R. D. (2011). A social capital framework for the study of institutional agents and their role in the empowerment of low-status students and youth. *Youth & Society*, *43*, 1066–1109.

Talburt, S., & Boyles, D. (2005). Reconsidering learning communities: Expanding the discourse by challenging the discourse. *Journal of General Education*, *54*(3), 209–236.

Weiss, M. J., Visher, M. G., Weissman, E., & Wathington, H. (2015). The impact of learning communities for students in developmental education: A synthesis of findings from randomized trials at six community colleges. *Educational Evaluation and Policy Analysis*, 1–22. doi:10.3102/0162373714563307

GLORIA CRISP *is an associate professor, College of Education, Oregon State University at Corvallis, Oregon.*

NEW DIRECTIONS FOR COMMUNITY COLLEGES • DOI: 10.1002/cc

Index

ORDER FORM SUBSCRIPTION AND SINGLE ISSUES

DISCOUNTED BACK ISSUES:

Use this form to receive 20% off all back issues of *New Directions for Community College*.
All single issues priced at **$23.20** (normally $29.00)

TITLE	ISSUE NO.	ISBN

Call 1-800-835-6770 or see mailing instructions below. When calling, mention the promotional code JBNND to receive your discount. For a complete list of issues, please visit www.wiley.com/WileyCDA/WileyTitle/productCd-CC.html

SUBSCRIPTIONS: (1 YEAR, 4 ISSUES)

☐ New Order   ☐ Renewal

U.S.	☐ Individual: $89	☐ Institutional: $356
CANADA/MEXICO	☐ Individual: $89	☐ Institutional: $398
ALL OTHERS	☐ Individual: $113	☐ Institutional: $434

Call 1-800-835-6770 or see mailing and pricing instructions below.
Online subscriptions are available at www.onlinelibrary.wiley.com

ORDER TOTALS:

Issue / Subscription Amount: $ _____

Shipping Amount: $ _____
(for single issues only – subscription prices include shipping)

Total Amount: $ _____

SHIPPING CHARGES:
First Item $6.00
Each Add'l Item $2.00

(No sales tax for U.S. subscriptions. Canadian residents, add GST for subscription orders. Individual rate subscriptions must be paid by personal check or credit card. Individual rate subscriptions may not be resold as library copies.)

BILLING & SHIPPING INFORMATION:

☐ **PAYMENT ENCLOSED:** *(U.S. check or money order only. All payments must be in U.S. dollars.)*

☐ **CREDIT CARD:** ☐VISA ☐MC ☐AMEX

Card number _____Exp. Date_____

Card Holder Name_____Card Issue #_____

Signature _____Day Phone_____

☐ **BILL ME:** *(U.S. institutional orders only. Purchase order required.)*

Purchase order # _____
                    Federal Tax ID 13559302 • GST 89102-8052

Name_____

Address_____

Phone_____ E-mail_____

Copy or detach page and send to: **John Wiley & Sons, Inc. / Jossey Bass**
PO Box 55381
Boston, MA 02205-9850

PROMO JBNND